MORKMON A QUARTERLY MODEL OF THE NETHERLANDS ECONOMY FOR MACRO-ECONOMIC POLICY ANALYSIS

MORKMON
A Quarterly Model of the Netherlands Economy for Macro-economic Policy Analysis

With a foreword of the president of the Bank

Monetary Monographs No. 2

1985 De Nederlandsche Bank n.v.
Martinus Nijhoff Publishers, Dordrecht

ISBN-13:978-90-247-3158-9 e-ISBN-13:978-94-009-5109-9
DOI:10.1007/978-94-009-5109-9

Distributors
For the United States and Canada: Kluwer Academic Publishers,
190 Old Derby Street, Hingham, MA 02043, USA
For the UK and Ireland: Kluwer Academic Publishers, MTP Press Limited, Falcon House,
Queen Square, Lancaster LA1 1RN, England
For all other countries: Kluwer Academic Publishers Group, Distribution Center,
P.O. Box 322, 3300 AH Dordrecht, The Netherlands

Foreword of the president

Economics attempts to explain, from a certain angle, the results of human behaviour. Economic policy attempts to influence it. Econometrics attempts to instil into both the theoretician and the policy maker greater discipline of thought by embodying the economic relationships in clear-cut quantified formulae. Mankind and the world are – fortunately, I am inclined to say – so complex that our understanding of reality, including economic reality, is never complete. By trial and error, we seek to understand and, if we think we have gained some understanding, to exert an influence. Postulates and instinct, theories and hunches, econometric models and the backs of envelopes will all make their urgent claims upon the policy maker but he will need them all.

This somewhat down-to-earth introduction to the integrated quarterly model of the monetary and real economic sectors of the Netherlands does not in any way detract from my admiration for the work embodied in this book, nor from a feeling of pride at writing this foreword. Fifteen years ago I had the privilege of advising the Governing Board of the Netherlands Bank about the importance of releasing a group of people from their day-to-day routine in order to enable them to undertake systematic scientific research in the monetary area. This has resulted in an ever-increasing flow of publications and has now culminated in the model MORKMON.

I view this *magnum opus* of the Econometric Research and Special Studies Department as a milestone of the Bank's quantitative research.

I do hope that this study will encourage further research, within and outside the Bank, thus contributing towards a better understanding of the economic phenomena in our society.

W.F. Duisenberg

Preface

Until the early 1970s monetary econometrics was virtually unexplored territory in the Netherlands. The Bank's econometric research, which I have had the privilege to direct since 1971, sought to map this territory gradually and thus to obtain the elements for building a monetary model for the Netherlands. As regards the research strategy, I opted for the performance of studies on specific aspects. The quarterly model MORKMON presented in this monograph may be regarded as the conclusion of this research programme.

When building the model and writing this monograph, I made heavy and unremitting demands on the staff of the Econometric Research and Special Studies Department. I owe a debt of gratitude to them all. The contributions made by four of them - F.A.G. den Butter, A.P. Huijser, P. Kramer and W.C. Boeschoten - deserve special mention.

Summer of 1984 M.M.G. Fase

Contents

1 Introductory remarks

1.1 Prolegomena

The present monograph presents a description of the 'MOnetaire-Reële Kwartaal-MOdel voor Nederland' (Monetary-Real Economic Quarterly Model for the Netherlands), which has been developed at the Netherlands Bank. The model, which is known by its acronym MORKMON, provides a systematic description of a number of relationships within the real economic sector on the one hand and the monetary sector on the other, as well of the links between the two sectors of the Netherlands economy. In this connection the question could arise why the Netherlands Bank has developed a model of its own, next to the existing models of the Dutch Central Planning Bureau. A number of answers are possible.

The first consideration was that for the Netherlands, until recently, there was no integrated model of the real economic and monetary sectors. Its development at the Bank was the logical sequel to the econometric research in the monetary area which had been conducted at the Bank since the early 1970s. Traces of this research into various monetary aspects are to be found in the formulation of the model. An added factor was that, in our opinion, a policy model may really come into its own when model builder and policy maker are living under the same roof. This permits the researcher to gain first-hand knowledge of the problems for which the policy maker will consult the model. Other reasons were the opportunities to include new information and recent figures and to incorporate institutional changes, which are frequent in the monetary sector in particular. The possibilities of tailoring the model to the Bank's specific policy areas and of permanent updating – often problematic for models developed elsewhere – were also among the underlying considerations. Furthermore, the availability of a model developed by the organization itself promotes coherence of policy analysis. Finally, it provides guidance for the in-house research in support of policy and stimulates a continued critical review of the organization's own products enabling them to be tested against actual policy needs. Ultimately, this was the principal motivation for undertaking the construction of the Bank's model. Fairly recently this view was expressed by the Bank's President in his contribution to the *liber amicorum* for the retiring Director of the Dutch Central Planning Bureau, Professor Van den Beld. In this contribution, which presents an overview of the similarities and differences between the monetary sub-models of the Bureau and the Bank, both published in 1981, the President noted that the main message model calculations offer to policy makers is [cf. Duisenberg (1984, p. 103)]:

'lines of march with information about expectable events or obstacles'

Earlier versions of the monetary block of the model described in the present monograph were published in 1981 and 1984 under the acronyms MOKMON-1-81 and MOKMON-1-82 [cf. Fase (1981a, 1984)]. The construction of this monetary block preceded that of the real economic sub-model, whose construction was initially hampered by a lack of a coherent set of quarterly figures. The first version of this real economic sub-model was described by Fase (1982). The need for data to elaborate the sub-model was the principal reason why the Bank has constructed and published confrontations of quarterly estimates of income and expenditure [cf. De Nederlandsche Bank N.V. (1982)]. The quarterly model presented in this monograph relies in part on these data. The monetary data are, of course, drawn from the statistics compiled by the Bank for a large number of years for purposes of policy analysis.

1.2 Organization

This publication primarily serves to present a description of the quantified economic relationships in MORKMON. Consequently, no lengthy discussions will be devoted to econometric refinements or to theoretical considerations underlying the postulated behavioural equations. Not only has the available theory been explored, it has also been exploited where necessary to find a plausible structure for the relevant relationships. As to the statistical analysis, ordinary least squares estimation methods have been used, although in some cases resort was had to more complex methods such as generalized least squares or seemingly unrelated regression techniques. A major consideration in this respect was the conviction that the primary purpose of a macro-economic model is to translate the variety of economic ideas in a coherent manner into a model structure lending itself to estimation. It stands to reason that we have sought to cause the model to reflect in full the interaction between theoretical desirability and empirical possibility. It is, however, uncertain whether the achievement of optimum interaction requires the use of the most sophisticated estimation methods. Consequently, for the time being we have refrained in this monograph – fully in line with usage in present-day model building – from focusing undue attention on the method of estimation.

The original intention was to estimate the model for the period 1970:I-1979:IV. However, various exceptions have been made, not only because more data became available as time progressed but also because in a number of cases situations arose which threw doubt upon the relationships established earlier. Consequently, in some cases the estimation period extends until 1982:IV, or begins in 1971 or even after 1971. It is neither efficient nor theoretically necessary for the estimation periods to be wholly identical. This may serve as an indication that the historical relationships should be revised from time to time.

Chapters 2, 3 and 4 present a description of the monetary block, the real economic block and the links between the two, respectively. On the basis of the results of dynamic model simulations, the *ex post* forecasting power is analysed in Chapter 5. In Chapter 6 impulse simulations are used to present the effects of a number of uncertainty and policy variants, as well as some sensitivity analyses. The concluding Chapter briefly reviews a number of criticisms regarding macro-economic modelling. Appendices I and II contain a complete description of the model and an explanation of the symbols used.

2 The relationships in the monetary sector

2.1 Balance sheets

As noted before, the monetary block discussed in this Chapter is an elaboration of earlier versions [see Fase (1981a, 1984)]. It is based on five balance sheets for the different sectors of the Netherlands economy. This balance sheet approach is in conformity with modern developments in monetary theory, where stocks are assigned a central position. In this view the flow quantities reflect the dynamics of stock adjustment.

The following sectors are distinguished:

. Private sector
. Money-creating institutions
. Central bank
. Government
. Rest of the world

The balance sheets of these sectors contain the assets and liabilities representing the structure of each of these sectors and, hence, of the economy as a whole. Such stylization offers a useful and general basis for monetary analysis. It is, moreover, closely in line with the Bank's long-standing statistical practice [cf. Imhülsen (1981)]. The following sections briefly describe the balance sheets used, with the relevant amounts at the end of 1979.

2.1.1 Private sector

The first items on the assets side of the private sector's balance sheet are the four components of the money stock: currency, CH, demand deposits, D, time deposits and foreign-currency deposits, TV, and the private sector's holdings of short-term government debt, KOS_{ps}. Savings deposits have been broken down into savings deposits with money-creating institutions, S_b, and savings deposits with institutional investors, S_{fs}. The latter item also figures on the liabilities side of the private sector's balance sheet. Similar incomplete consolidation of the institutional investors in the private sector's balance sheet occurs in respect of the item $LK_{fs,gb}$, long-term lending by institutional investors to households and enterprises. The reasons for this incomplete consolidation will be discussed later.

In this balance sheet, the private sector's holdings of foreign liabilities are included in BNIB. This item is marked by a very heterogeneous composition, comprising

Private sector's balance sheet
(billions of guilders)

	1979		*1979*
CH	20.0	BL	71.8
D	42.2	$LK_{b,ps}$	104.7
TV	39.1	$LK_{fs,gb}$	111.0
KOS_{ps}	2.1	S_{fs}	37.4
S_b	77.8	BBIN	69.8
S_{fs}	37.4	LB_{lo}	2.7
$LK_{ps,b}$	32.7	V_{ps}	149.9
$LK_{ps,o}$	100.3		
$LK_{fs,gb}$	111.0		
BNIB	84.8		
	547.4		547.4

foreign securities, deposits held abroad, intra-group loans and accumulated outward direct investment as well as real estate. The level of BNIB has been approximated by cumulating recorded capital flows since 1960.

As to the assets side of the private sector's balance sheet, the following remark may be made with regard to the figures shown. Comparison of the balance sheet total at end-1979 with that of Fl. 722.4 billion at end-1982 reveals an increase of 32 %. In the same period, the growth of the money stock, M2, was less than 20 %. Long-term lending, however, increased by nearly 40 %, with a very striking expansion – a more than 60 % growth – of lending to the government. This means that, within the limits of the stylization used, the structure of the private sector's balance sheet shows no signs whatever of rigidity. This provides additional grounds for describing this balance sheet structure by means of economically founded behavioural equations.

On the liabilities side, short-term bank lending, BL, which totalled Fl. 71.8 billion in 1979, was substantially smaller than the Fl. 215 billion of long-term funds borrowed by the private sector from all financial institutions combined, consisting of $LK_{fs,gb}$, already mentioned, and $LK_{b,ps}$. The former represents the long-term funds borrowed from the non-money-creating institutions, the latter the funds borrowed from the money-creating banking system. The item BBIN relates to foreign holdings of domestic liabilities and comprises, in principle, the same components as the asset item BNIB. The balance of the two constitutes the private sector's net foreign assets. At the end of 1979, the private sector thus held net foreign assets amounting to Fl. 84.8 billion minus Fl. 69.8 billion equals Fl. 15.0 billion, being BNIB – BBIN. As will be shown later, LB_{lo} is an asset item in the government's balance sheet, consisting largely of deposits with the money-creating institutions. In the private sector's balance sheet, the money stock as a whole figures on the assets side. Consequently, the item LB_{lo} is included as a liability in the private sector's balance sheet and serves to adjust the total money stock as far as it is not held by the private sector. Finally, V_{ps} represents the net financial wealth of the private sector and effectuates balance sheet equality for this sector.

2.1.2 Money-creating institutions

In the same way as for the private sector, the basis for the description of this sector is formed by the aggregate balance sheet (excluding the central bank).

As may be expected from a coherent system of balance sheets, the money-creating institutions' balance sheet includes various assets and liabilities also shown in the private sector's balance sheet. An asset not encountered before is VR, which amounted to a mere Fl. 11 million at end-1979. It represents the banking system's balances held at the central bank; the banking system uses them as working balances. Net foreign assets, NBA_b, comprises the banking system's foreign assets and liabilities. At end-1979, there were net foreign liabilities of Fl. 340 million. The small amount of this *net* item at that particular date is fortuitous and masks the major role which this item plays in the banks' balance sheet, not least on account of its fluctuations. For example, at end-1975 NBA_b was nearly Fl. 7 billion, whereas end-1980 showed a net foreign liability position of nearly the same amount.

Money-creating institutions' balance sheet
(billions of guilders)

	1979		*1979*
VR	0.0	GLR	5.6
NBA_b	-0.3	D	42.2
BL	71.8	TV	39.1
KOS_b	20.3	S_b	77.8
$LK_{b,ps}$	104.7	$LK_{ps,b}$	32.7
$LK_{b,o}$	13.9	KT_{ro}	0.8
DA_b	20.4	V_b	32.6
	230.8		230.8

Holdings of short-term government debt, KOS_b, which include mainly Treasury paper, totalled Fl. 20.3 billion at end-1979. Long-term lending to the government, represented by $LK_{b,o}$, was Fl. 13.9 billion at end-1979, but rose to over Fl. 23 billion at end-1982. A new item on the liabilities side is GLR, the so-called borrowed reserves at the central bank, totalling Fl. 5.6 billion at end-1979. This item includes bills, promissory notes, Treasury paper and debt instruments sold to the central bank at a discount as well as the advances and special loans obtained from the central bank. The item KT_{ro} represents the central government's deposits with the banking system; at Fl. 817 million at end-1979, it is of minor significance. The final item, V_b, the banking system's net wealth, ensures balance sheet equality.

2.1.3 *Central bank*

The central bank's balance sheet is published weekly. The balance sheet presented here is a stylized version of this weekly return.

The item borrowed reserves, GLR, which comprises the central bank's claims on the private banking system, including special loans, was already discussed. Through

Central bank's balance sheet
(billions of guilders)

	1979		*1979*
GLR	5.6	CH_{cb}	19.0
KOS_{cb}	0.5	VR	0.0
$LK_{cb,o}$	0.5	SSCH	2.3
IR	23.6	V_{cb}	8.9
	30.2		30.2

the interest rate charged, this item provides the central bank with one of the instruments to implement its policy towards the banking system. The item KOS_{cb} largely consists of the holdings of Netherlands coin, thus representing a claim on the central government. Totalling Fl. 23.6 billion at end-1979, the gold and foreign exchange holdings, represented here by IR, are the largest single item on the assets side of the central bank's balance sheet. The largest item on the liabilities side is CH_{cb}, the outstanding amount of bank notes, which totalled Fl. 19.0 billion at end-1979. The Treasury's balance, SSCH, was Fl. 2.3 billion at end-1979. The central bank's net wealth, V_{cb}, which includes the revaluations of the gold and foreign exchange holdings and the reserves, aggregated Fl. 8.9 billion at end-1979. This item effectuates balance sheet equality.

2.1.4 *Government*

Although each year's Budget Memorandum includes a balance sheet for the central government, the present study employs an artificial balance sheet for the government

– including the local government – arranged along the same lines as the other balance sheets used. At the heart of this balance sheet are the accumulated financial surpluses and deficits $\sum_{\tau=0}^{t} (FT_o)_\tau$, where $(FT_o)_\tau$ represents the financial balance in period τ, with $\tau=0$ for the initial period and $\tau=t$ for the most recent period. For the sake of brevity, this accumulated financial surplus is noted below as ΣFT_o.

Government's balance sheet
(billions of guilders)

	1979		*1979*
ΣFT_o	130.5	CH_{ro}	1.0
LB_{lo}	2.7	KOS_{ps}	2.1
KT_{ro}	0.8	$LK_{ps,o}$	100.3
SSCH	2.3	KOS_b	20.3
NBA_o	2.3	$LK_{b,o}$	13.9
		KOS_{cb}	0.5
		$LK_{cb,o}$	0.5
	138.6		138.6

The balance sheet shows, in principle, the manner in which the accumulated financial deficits have been financed. Additionally, it includes a number of relatively minor items, viz liquid assets held by the local government, LB_{lo}, deposits with banks, KT_{ro}, the Treasury's balance at the central bank, SSCH, and the government's net foreign assets, NBA_o. The liabilities side shows the sources of finance, with long-term lending by the private sector, $LK_{ps,o}$, as the principal component. The least important item in quantitative terms, one not discussed before, is coin in circulation, CH_{ro}. Together with the bank notes in circulation, CH_{cb}, shown in the central bank's balance sheet, this constitutes the currency circulation, CH.

2.1.5 *Rest of the world*

Like the government's balance sheet, the foreign sector's balance sheet is artificial. The usual description of external relationships is provided by the balance of payments, which is, however, expressed in terms of flows instead of stocks as required here. Using the accumulated balances on current account, $\sum_{\tau=0}^{t} LR_\tau$, it is possible to compile a balance sheet of the foreign sector (LR_τ is the balance on current account in period τ and t the most recent period).

The assets side includes two items representing accumulated balance-of-payments quantities: the current-account surplus or deficit on a cash basis, LR, and the items in transit and other exogenous items on the balance of payments on a cash basis, RBO. The liabilities side comprises the items which reflect the accumulation of surpluses, measured on a cash basis: the gold and foreign exchange holdings, IR, and the net foreign assets of the government, NBA_o, the banks, NBA_b, and the private sector, $NBA_{ps} = BNIB - BBIN$. It should be noted that in this set-up the private sector's net foreign assets, NBA_{ps}, have not been included as the balance of assets and liabilities. The foreign assets and liabilities, represented by BNIB and BBIN, respectively, have been distinguished in view of the model structure used. The private sector's net foreign assets, incidentally, increased from Fl. 15.0 billion at end-1979 to Fl. 24.5 billion in 1982; as discussed later, this was especially due to the persistent balance-of-payments surpluses recorded after 1980.

Foreign sector's balance sheet
(billions of guilders)

	1979		*1979*
ΣLR	19.4	IR	23.6
ΣRBO	15.0	NBA_b	-0.3
ΣNBARV	6.1	NBA_o	2.3
BBIN	69.8	BNIB	84.8
	110.3		110.3

2.2 Balance sheet constraints

The system of balance sheets described above constitutes the framework for the monetary model. It is, therefore, useful to review the interrelationship of these balance sheets. To that end, Table 2.1 summarizes the balance sheets and presents a coherent picture of the intersectoral assets and liabilities. The Table also shows the principal interest rates included in the model. Table 2.1 offers three opportunities to gain an insight into the monetary sub-model and its connection with the Bank's practice of monetary analysis.

Firstly, it is easy to see that, measured in terms of changes, the assets and liabilities Table corresponds to a detailed financing summary, as traditionally published in the Bank's Annual Reports. Such a summary presents, on the one hand, the financial surpluses and deficits by sector, represented here by the changes in item 19, and, on the other, the manner in which these surpluses or deficits are used or financed, respectively. These financial surpluses and deficits constitute the accounting link with the real economic sector. Consequently, expressed in terms of changes, item 19 of Table

Table 2.1
Intersectoral assets and liabilities

	private sector	institutional investors	money-creating institutions
1. Currency	CH		
2. Demand deposits	D		-D
3. Time deposits and foreign-currency deposits	TV		-TV
4. Savings deposits	S	$-S_{fs}$	$-S_b$
5. Treasury's balance			
6. Central government's cash and deposits			$-KT_{ro}$
7. Liquid assets held by the local government	$-LB_{lo}$		
8. Short-term government debt	KOS_{ps}		KOS_b
9. Banks' balances			VR
10. Banks' borrowed reserves			-GLR
11. Short-term bank lending to the private sector	-BL		BL
12. Long-term funds raised from the private sector by the banks	$LK_{ps,b}$		$-LK_{ps,b}$
13. Long-term lending to the private sector	$-LOG_{ps}$	$LK_{fs,gb}$	$LK_{b,ps}$
14. Long-term lending to the government	$LK_{ps,o}$		$LK_{b,o}$
15. Gold and foreign exchange holdings			
16. Other holdings of foreign liabilities	BNIB		NBA_b
17. Foreign holdings of domestic liabilities	-BBIN		
18. Miscellaneous bank assets			DA_b
19. Wealth/accumulated financial surplus and deficits	$-V_{ps}$		$-V_b$

Explanatory note:
Assets + sign, liabilities − sign; the column institutional investors has been included to illustrate the effects of the partial consolidation with the private sector.

2.1 corresponds to the well-known macro-economic budget constraint that the government's financial deficit, the balance on current account, E, and the private sector's savings surplus, $S_p - I$, sum to zero:

$$\Delta V_{ps} + \Delta V_b + \Delta V_{cb} - FT_o - LR = S_p - I - FT_o^{tr} - E = 0$$

The *ad hoc* symbol S_p represents total savings and ΔV_{ps} may also be taken to represent the private sector's savings surplus.

Viewed from a financial angle, Table 2.1 shows the balance sheet contraints typical of any monetary model based on balance sheets. In this case, there are four contraints, the fifth being implied by the other four because, mathematically, it is not an inde-

government	central bank	rest of the world	interest rates
$-CH_{ro}$	$-CH_{cb}$		
			r_d, r_{M2}
			r_{TV}
			r_s
SSCH	-SSCH		
KT_{ro}			
LB_{lo}			
-KOS	KOS_{cb}		r_k, r_{sc}
	-VR		
	GLR		
			r_{bl}
			r_l
-VAS	$LK_{cb,o}$		
	IR	-IR	
NBA_o		$-(NBA_b+NBA_o$ $+BNIB)$	
		BBIN	
		$\Sigma(RBO+NBARV)$	
ΣFT_o	$-V_{cb}$	ΣLR	

pendent equation. The balance sheet equality of the central bank has been chosen as the implicit constraint. The balance sheet equalities explicitly allowed for in the model, as well as the ensuing balance sheet equality for the central bank, are shown in Table 2.2.

A third aspect of Table 2.1 is that it gives an overview of the financial markets described in the monetary sub-model. For each of the various financial assets, the equality of supply and demand is shown explicitly.

Table 2.2
Balance sheet equalities in the monetary sub-model

private sector:

(1) $FA = BL + LOG_{ps} + S_{fs} + V_{ps} + LB_{lo} + BBIN$

money-creating institutions:

(16) $VR + NBA_b + BL + KOS_b + LK_b + DA_b = D + TV + S_b + LK_{ps,b} + $
$+ GLR + KT_{ro} + V_b$

government:

(45) $SSCH = SSCH_{-1} + (\delta_1 + \delta_2 - 1) FT_o^*$

rest of the world:

(47) $\Delta IR = LR + RBO + NBARV - \Delta NBA_{ps} - \Delta NBA_b - \Delta NBA_o$

(implicit balance sheet equality of the) central bank:

$GLR + KOS_{cb} + LK_{cb,o} + IR = CH_{cb} + VR + SSCH + V_{cb}$

2.3 The monetary model in outline

The balance sheet items, or their changes, described above are the key variables of the monetary sub-model. These quantities, unless determined exogenously, and the relevant interest and exchange rates, are the variables to be explained by the model. As a result, the monetary sub-model comprises over 50 equations. Half of these are behavioural equations. The aggregation of the balance sheet items in the model corresponds with the usual analysis of macro-economic financial behaviour in the theoretical and empirical literature. Most of the financial behavioural equations concerned have, incidentally, been the subject of earlier research at the Bank. In this sense, the monetary sub-model, like its predecessors, is to be regarded as the provisional conclusion and the systematic integration of empirical monetary research conducted earlier at the Bank.

In the monetary model, the behavioural explanation of the balance sheet items focuses on the private sector. Following up research into the total demand for money [see Fase and Kuné (1974); Den Butter and Fase (1981)] or its components [see Fase (1977, 1978, 1979b)], attention is paid to the determinants of the private sector's demand for liquid assets. The model describes the private sector's portfolio behaviour with regard to all assets combined. In this approach the money stock, as part of the total financial portfolio, is made dependent on national income as a proxy for the volume of transactions. Thus, an essential characteristic of the usual demand-for-money analysis has been retained in the portfolio or allocation model. Moreover, this allows consideration of various monetary aggregates without abandoning a central concept of liquidity.

Another aggregate explained by means of the private sector's portfolio behaviour is savings deposits. Though consisting of savings deposits with banks and savings deposits with institutional investors, the two are combined in the behavioural equation as it makes no difference to the holders where they hold their savings. This also explains why the savings deposits with institutional investors have not been consolidated in the private sector's balance sheet, but are shown separately.

In addition to long-term domestic investments, the behavioural model for the private sector's financial assets includes holdings of foreign liabilities, BNIB. By contrast with earlier versions of the monetary model and earlier research at the Bank [see Koning (1974)], the present model considers *gross* instead of *net* capital transactions [cf. also Huijser (1984)]. This approach ensues from the fact that the allocation model employed in this monograph explicitly describes the choice between domestic and foreign assets. Consequently, a separate behavioural equation must be included for foreign holdings of domestic liabilities, BBIN.

The principal behavioural equations on the liabilities side of the private sector's balance sheet concern the demand for short-term bank loans and the demand for long-term funds. The demand for short-term bank loans was investigated earlier by Fase (1979a), while a major component of the demand for long-term funds, mortgage credit, was researched by Den Butter, Dongelmans and Fase (1977). In line with these earlier studies, the lending has been related in both demand-for-credit equations to appropriate scale variables from the real economic sector. This construction allows divergency between the demand for credit, and hence this component of the supply of money, and the income-dependent demand for money resulting from the movements in the scale variable concerned. The model describes how the resulting tension is reflected in the monetary sector through the allocation model for the financial assets or through interest rates. A model which would merely consider net (long-term) lending would not permit such insight into this mechanism.

In regard of the demand for long-term credit, the same phenomenon occurs as that noted above for savings deposits: for the borrowers it makes no appreciable difference whether they raise their long-term funds from the banks or from the institutional investors. Consequently, long-term lending by institutional investors to households and enterprises, $LK_{fs,gb}$, has not been consolidated in the private sector's balance sheet. Moreover, if such lending were consolidated, the model would ignore the major role played in the capital market by the institutional investors. On the other hand, the institutional investors have not been included as a fully independent sector. Although this would have been possible, we have hitherto refrained from doing so in order to avoid both data problems and undue model complexity.

Together with the gross demand for credit and with foreign capital, the accumulated savings surplus of the private sector, which, as noted above, follows from the macro-economic budget constraint, governs the private sector's supply of financial assets. This supply is allocated among the various assets in accordance with the afore-mentioned portfolio model.

In the money-creating institutions' balance sheet, the balance sheet items are explained to a much lesser extent than in the private sector's balance sheet from the (portfolio) behaviour of these institutions. Apart from the items already explained in the context of the private sector's balance sheet, the principal behavioural equation here concerns the banks' net foreign assets, NBA_b. Its specification has been derived from Den Butter, Fase and Huijser (1979), who investigated the extent to which, in addition to the banks' behaviour, the banks' customers and the central bank's policy affect this balance sheet item. On the grounds of this earlier research, it has been assumed in the present model that the banks themselves exert only a very modest influence on their net foreign assets. On the other hand, the banks' behaviour does play an important role in the equations determining the allocation of savings deposits and long-term funds raised between the banks and the institutional investors. Additionally, the banks' behaviour is reflected in the model through their price setting of the financial assets relevant to the banks. The model thus describes the banks' influence on their portfolio composition in an indirect manner.

Apart from its afore-mentioned effect on the banks' net foreign assets, the central bank's policy has been modelled by means of a number of behavioural equations comprising the discount on promissory notes and credit restriction policy as their determinants. Moreover, the short-term interest rate follows from a reaction function reflecting the central bank's money and foreign exchange market policies. This approach has been inspired by earlier research by Fase and Huijser (1980) and Huijser (1980).

In the government's balance sheet, the government's financing behaviour is described.

Apart from the current-account surplus or deficit on a cash basis, the accumulated balance of payments does not include any balance sheet items which are eligible for explanation by means of a behavioural equation in the monetary sub-model. The current account on a transactions basis is, of course, determined in the real economic sub-model. Thus, the monetary sub-model includes two equations for trade credit, which endogenize the difference between the current account on a transactions basis and that on a cash basis. The equations describe the behaviour of foreign and domestic suppliers and customers. Earlier research in this area was conducted by Van Nieuwkerk (1978).

Finally, the model describes the long-term interest rate. If the banks' portfolio behaviour were described explicitly in the model, this interest rate would follow implicitly from the equality of supply and demand in the capital market. As noted above, this approach was not chosen to describe the banks' behaviour. A major argument against it was the fact that the money market rate would then also be explained by means of the equality of supply and demand in the money market. However, as the money market rate is largely governed by the central bank's policy, preference has been given to modelling this rate by means of a reaction function. Consequently, in regard of the capital market rate, a behavioural equation has been specified, from which this rate follows explicitly. In addition to factors related to price setting behaviour of both lenders and borrowers, this interest rate equation includes the tension in the capital market as a determinant. Thus, the equation is, in a sense, given the character of a reduced form.

The essence of the monetary sub-model outlined above is summarized in the form of a flow diagram in Chart 2.1. The black arrows show the interaction between monetary variables. The broken arrows represent the influence in the monetary sector exerted by the real economic sector, by policy and by the rest of the world. The diagram shows that in the model the supply of financial assets stems from three sources, viz the rest of the world, the banking system and the government. This is in line with the Bank's usual analysis. The demand for financial assets, including money, is governed by interest rates and by developments in the real economic sector. Imbalances between supply and demand are reflected in the capital market, influencing interest rates and supply from the rest of the world. The latter primarily depends on the long-term interest rate and on exchange rates.

The above outline of the model cannot, and is not intended to, afford any insight into details. Such an insight demands a discussion of the individual model equations, which are shown in Appendix I, equations (1) to (52). The symbols are explained in Appendix II.

2.4 The behavioural equations for the monetary sector

The behavioural equations can be presented in any of various ways. An obvious system would be classification by sector. Another possibility is classification by corresponding groups of financial assets or liabilities which mostly relate to at least two of the sectors distinguished. In line with earlier publications [cf. Fase (1981a, 1984)], a presentation from a more economic point of view has been preferred to the sectoral accounting alternative.

2.4.1 Demand for financial assets

2.4.1.1 Portfolio behaviour model

The demand for financial assets stems mainly from households and enterprises, determining the assets side of the private sector's balance sheet. The portfolio behaviour model presents an economically justified and proved instrument to describe the underlying behaviour. Formulated in general terms, such a model is as follows. It con-

Chart 2.1
Flow diagram of the monetary block of MORKMON

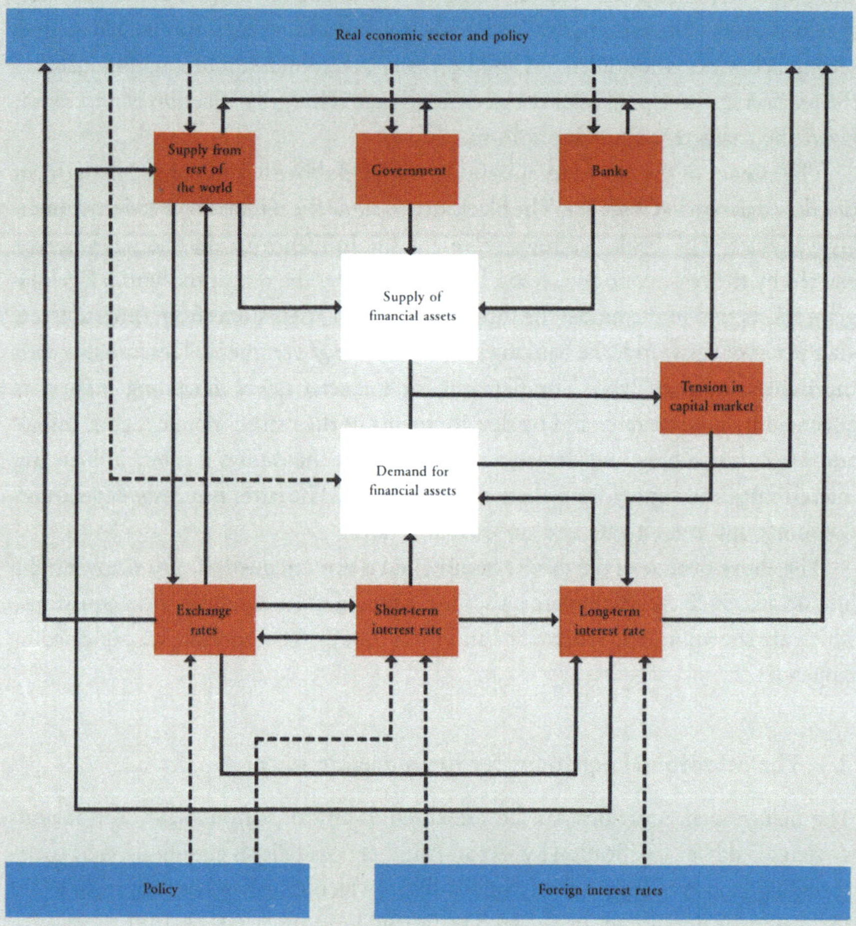

cerns a financial asset A_i with $\Sigma_i A_i = A$. Apart from stochastics, the following behavioural equation is postulated for the share of this asset A_i in the total asset portfolio A_i/A:

$$\frac{A_i^*}{A} = \alpha_{io} + \Sigma_j \alpha_{ij} r_j + \Sigma_l \beta_{il} X_l \tag{1}$$

where r_j represents interest rates, X_l other explanatory variables, and A_i^*/A the optimum or desirable share of asset i in the total portfolio A. Because $\Sigma_i A_i^*/A = 1$, it follows that $\sum_{i=1}^{n} \alpha_{ij} = \sum_{i=1}^{n} \beta_{il} = 0$ and $\sum_{i=1}^{n} \alpha_{io} = 1$. Finally, symmetry has been assumed for the interest rate coefficient α_{ij}, so that $\alpha_{ij} = \alpha_{ji}$ for all cases where $i \neq j$ [cf. e.g. Brainard and Tobin (1968); Fase (1979b)].

Furthermore, a partial adjustment mechanism has been assumed:

$$\Delta A_i = \Sigma_h \lambda_{ih} (A_h^* - A_{h_{-1}}) \tag{2}$$

where $\Sigma_i \lambda_{ih} = 1$ for all values of h. Substitution of (1) into the scaled equation (2) results in:

$$\frac{\Delta A_i}{A} = \Sigma_h - \lambda_{ih} \frac{A_{h_{-1}}}{A} + \Sigma_h \lambda_{ih} \alpha_{ho} + \Sigma_j (\Sigma_h \lambda_{ih} \alpha_{hj}) r_j + \Sigma_l (\Sigma_h \lambda_{ih} \beta_{hl}) X_l$$

or, in a simplified form:

$$\frac{\Delta A_i}{A} = \Sigma_h - \lambda_{ih} \frac{A_{h_{-1}}}{A} + \pi_{io} + \Sigma_j \pi_{ij} r_j + \Sigma_l \pi_{il} X_l \tag{3}$$

Model (3) has been estimated subject to the above-mentioned constraints regarding α, β and λ after addition of assumptions regarding stochastics.

The application of model (3) in this context involved, firstly, a description of the allocation of the private sector's balance sheet total, FA, among four general categories, viz the money stock, M2, the private sector's savings deposits, S, the long-term domestic investments – comprising mainly bonds and private loans –, LK_{ps}, and the private sector's holdings of foreign liabilities, BNIB. Secondly, using a basically analogous model, the aggregate M2 (the money stock) was allocated among its components, viz currency, CH, demand deposits, D, time deposits including liquid savings deposits and foreign-currency deposits of residents, TV, and short-term government debt held by the private sector, KOS_{ps}. On the basis of the assets side of the private sector's balance sheet described in section 2.1.1, this two-stage allocation may be summarized as shown in Table 2.3.

Table 2.3
Private sector's balance sheet

		CH		BL
	M2	D	$LK_{b,ps}$	LOG_{ps}
		TV	$LK_{fs,gb}$	
		KOS_{ps}		
	S	S_b		S_{fs}
		S_{fs}		
FA				BBIN
		$LK_{ps,b}$		
	LK_{ps}	$LK_{ps,o}$		LB_{lo}
		$LK_{fs,gb}$		V_{ps}
	BNIB			
		FA		FA

2.4.1.2 Empirical elaboration for financial assets

Firstly, the portfolio behaviour model was estimated for the allocation of total assets, FA, among the four components for the period 1970:III-1982:IV using the joint least squares method with restrictions. Estimation was done in two stages. The first consisted of estimation of the coefficients of adjustment, λ, which are presented in Table 2.4. The t-values are given in parentheses.

The results show that four of the sixteen coefficients have been set at zero; during estimation, it became evident that otherwise they would have assumed wrong signs. The own-speed of adjustment of M2 is considerably higher than those of S and LK_{ps}. This is wholly in agreement with the degree of liquidity of this asset. At 0.54, the own-coefficient of adjustment of BNIB is in between the two extremes. BNIB comprises items having widely varying degrees of liquidity: current-account deposits, money market investments, short and long-term credits, securities, loans, direct investment and real estate (all of them abroad). Considering the significance of BNIB's liquid components, the coefficient of adjustment found would appear to be fully acceptable.

It follows from the so-called cross effects, which are also shown in Table 2.4, that M2 apparently performs an important transmitting function, which is particularly

Table 2.4
Estimation results for the coefficients of adjustment in the portfolio behaviour model for financial assets

	$M2_{-1}/FA$	S_{-1}/FA	$LK_{ps_{-1}}/FA$	$BNIB_{-1}/FA$
$\Delta M2/FA$	-0.7572 (6.06)	-0.6622 (4.44)	-0.3993 (3.66)	0
$\Delta S/FA$	0	-0.2642 (3.39)	0	-0.3241 (1.93)
$\Delta LK_{ps}/FA$	-0.0914 (1.66)	0	-0.2998 (3.09)	-0.1363 (0.83)
$\Delta BNIB/FA$	-0.1513 (1.28)	-0.0737 (0.55)	-0.3009 (3.34)	-0.5396 (3.88)
Σ	-1	-1	-1	-1

Explanatory note:
Strictly speaking, the speed of adjustment is λ_{ih}; the Table shows $-\lambda_{ih}$.

evident in the case of savings deposits, for which a cross effect of 0.66 was found. According to the estimates, part of the funds intended for as yet unrealized or potential investments in long-term capital is apparently held abroad (30 %). Part of the funds intended for investments abroad is temporarily held in LK_{ps} (14 %) and S (32 %) but, according to the relevant estimates in Table 2.4, curiously enough not in M2. It stands to reason that in the long run the speeds of adjustment no longer play a role.

Secondly, conditional upon the speeds of adjustment discussed above, the other parameters were estimated. The results are shown in Table 2.5; the t-values are again given in parentheses. This allocation model distinguishes four interest rates of the respective financial assets. The assets' 'own' interest rate coefficients all have the sign expected on the basis of economic theory. Because estimation yielded the wrong sign for three of the cross coefficients of interest rates, the long-term coefficient was set at zero in these cases. Owing to the symmetry constraints, this meant that, only six out of twelve cross coefficients needed to be estimated. In order to compare these results with empirical results of others, the long-term elasticities have been calculated. The long-term elasticities of the interest rates, which are shown in Table 2.6, correspond fairly well to those in the literature [cf. e.g. Conrad (1980); Fase (1979b); Helliwell *et al.* (1971); Van Loo (1983); Saito (1977); Taylor and Clements (1983)].

Table 2.5 also shows the estimates for the coefficients of the other variables from model (3), the X_l. Gross national product Y_{bnpm} – with a coefficient α as a dummy variable for the 1977 break in series in the National Accounts – has been included in the model as an explanatory variable for the demand for M2 representing the transactions motive. On the basis of earlier research, a long-term demand elasticity of 0.95 has been assumed *a priori*. The variable $\Delta cadm \equiv \Delta[(e_{DM}-\bar{e}_{DM})/\bar{e}_{DM}]$ represents expected appreciation, which may influence BNIB in particular. The utilization rate of capital, q_k, acts as cyclical indicator, representing the effect of hoarding or

Table 2.5
Estimation results for the other coefficients of the portfolio behaviour model for financial assets under the symmetry and zero constraints

	r_{M2}	r_s	r_l	r_l^{bu}	$Y_{bnpm}\cdot\alpha_1/FA$	$\Delta cadm$
$\Delta M2/FA$	0.002499 (5.77)	-0.000553 (4.97)	-0.000020 (0.03)	-0.001926 (3.62)	0.24350 (5.46)	-0.00778 (0.20)
$\Delta S/FA$	-0.001537 (4.97)	0.001536 (4.97)	-0.001563 (3.62)	0.001563 (3.62)	0.08982 (1.96)	0.04309 (1.18)
$\Delta LK_{ps}/FA$	-0.000601 (3.04)	-0.000532 (4.97)	0.001921 (6.01)	-0.000788 (3.61)	-0.28151 (8.14)	-0.05441 (2.32)
$\Delta BNIB/FA$	-0.000361 (2.52)	-0.000451 (4.97)	-0.000338 (0.98)	0.001152 (3.62)	-0.05181 (1.77)	0.01910 (1.06)
Σ	0	0	0	0	0	0

Table 2.6
Long-term effects in the portfolio behaviour model for financial assets

	coefficients					
	r_{M2}	r_s	r_l	r_l^{bu}	$Y_{bnpm}\cdot\alpha_1/FA$	q_k
M2/FA	0.0113	-0.0058	-0.0054	0	1.27	-0.04
S/FA	-0.0058	0.0058	0	0	-0.17	0
LK_{ps}/FA	-0.0054	0	0.0103	-0.0048	-1.52	0.14
BNIB/FA	0	0	-0.0048	0.0048	0.42	-0.10

* Calculated for the values of the variables in 1982:IV.

dishoarding of liquid assets induced by the turning of the economic tide. Strictly speaking, this means that the transactions velocity of circulation of the money stock has been assumed to be variable. Owing to the system approach used, this assumption affects the other financial assets, albeit, logically, with varying signs.

Additionally, ΔBBIN/FA has been included as an explanatory variable in order to cope with the dynamics of the allocation of the financial assets. The estimation results in Table 2.5 show that an inflow of capital from abroad, represented in ΔBBIN, finds its way notably to S, LK_{ps} and BNIB, but not to any significant extent to the money

			seasonal dummies				
q_k	ΔBBIN/FA	dumb6	d_1	d_2	d_3	constant	standard error of residuals
0.02706 (2.87)	−0.41132 (2.64)	0.00576 (3.59)	0.00663 (5.98)	0.00790 (6.69)	0.00382 (3.48)	0.3969 (59.56)	0.0032
−0.03366 (5.11)	0.02800 (19.49)	−0.00739 (4.91)	0.00174 (1.68)	0.00049 (0.45)	0.00026 (0.25)	0.1226 (23.99)	0.0031
0.02537 (3.64)	0.21300 (2.31)	0.00087 (0.79)	−0.00345 (5.04)	−0.00381 (5.32)	−0.00316 (4.75)	0.1971 (41.47)	0.0021
−0.01877 (0.39)	0.17032 (0.23)	0.00077 (0.85)	−0.00491 (9.30)	−0.00458 (8.22)	−0.00092 (1.78)	0.2834 (83.97)	0.0015
0	0	0	0	0	0	1	

elasticities*					
r_{M2}	r_s	r_l	r_l^{bu}	$Y_{bnpm} \cdot \alpha_1$/FA	q_k
0.30	−0.22	−0.29	0	0.95	−0.19
−0.13	0.18	0	0	−0.11	0
−0.05	0	0.20	−0.10	−0.41	0.26
0	0	−0.27	0.29	0.32	−0.53

stock M2. Incidentally, $\Delta\Delta$FA, another and more general measure for an unexpected increase in wealth than ΔBBIN, proved to have no significant influence.

In summary, the description in this subsection shows that the allocation model for the private sector's financial assets must be estimated under a total of 24 constraints, viz 13 additivity constraints, 6 symmetry constraints, 3 zero constraints for cross coefficients of interest rates, one constraint regarding the long-term elasticity of Y_{bnpm} in the equation of M2 and one zero constraint regarding the long-term elasticity of q_k in the equation of S. It might be noted that considerations of economic theory have been the main argument for the last two constraints in particular.

2.4.1.3 Empirical elaboration for the money stock

The allocation of the money stock M2 among currency, CH, demand deposits, D, time deposits, including liquid savings, and foreign-currency deposits, TV, and short-term government debt held by the private sector, KOS_{ps}, is also described by means of the dynamic allocation model (3) used earlier. The model was again estimated in two rounds. Firstly, the coefficients of adjustment were determined. Subsequently, on the basis of the values thus found, the coefficients of the other explanatory variables were estimated subject to the various constraints.

The coefficients of adjustment are listed in Table 2.7. For currency, partly because of its liquid character, full adjustment within one quarter has been assumed. As a consequence of this constraint, the coefficients of CH_{-1}/M2 in the other equations become zero. The cross effects in the CH equation, which assumed the wrong sign in the first estimation, were set equal to zero. The own-coefficient of adjustment of the time deposits, which originally showed a value of 1.18, has been set at 0.80. This causes the own-speed of adjustment of demand deposits to increase from 0.64 to 0.84. The liquid character of the assets has been regarded as the principal determinant of their speed of adjustment. Other factors which may affect the length of the Koyck lags have been ignored here.

Table 2.8 presents the estimation results for the coefficients of the other variables. The estimates meet the constraints imposed on the system to ensure consistency. In cases where estimation of the long-term effects yielded the wrong sign, the relevant coefficients have been set equal to zero. The long-term effects of the explanatory variables are listed in Table 2.9. With regard to this Table, the following may be noted:

- Inflation has been interpreted as negative interest on currency and has been taken into account when imposing symmetry constraints upon the interest rates. As expected, an increase in the rate of inflation leads to a decrease in the share of currency, in favour of the share of interest-bearing time deposits.

Table 2.7
Estimation results for the coefficients of adjustment in the portfolio behaviour model for the money stock

	$CH_{-1}/M2$	$D_{-1}/M2$	$TV_{-1}/M2$	$KOS_{ps_{-1}}/M2$
$\Delta CH/M2$	-1	0	0	0
$\Delta D/M2$	0	-0.84432	-0.15486	-0.32580
		(8.90)	(4.47)	(1.43)
$\Delta TV/M2$	0	-0.09549	-0.8	-0.24875
		(1.00)		(1.05)
$\Delta KOS_{ps}/M2$	0	-0.06019	-0.04514	-0.42544
		(1.17)	(1.30)	(3.72)
Σ	-1	-1	-1	-1

Explanatory note:
Strictly speaking, the speed of adjustment is λ_{ih}; the Table shows $-\lambda_{ih}$.

- The interest rate effects found are approximately one-third of those found in MOKMON-1-82 [1]. They are also lower than the interest rate effects in the FREIA and KOMPAS models of the Dutch Central Planning Bureau. However, no full comparison is possible, as the allocated totals differ for the various models. Furthermore, the change in definition introduced at the end of 1977 has led to a decreased interest rate sensitivity of time deposits. Consequently, estimates relating to a more recent observation period will show a lesser effect of the short-term interest rate in particular.
- The reciprocal of M2 has been included in view of possible inhomogeneity of the system. An increase in the money stock leads to a larger share of time deposits and, to a lesser extent, of demand deposits.
- The income variable, which has been included on account of the transactions motive, has the expected influence; an increase in this variable leads to a shift from less liquid to more liquid assets.
- Finally, a dummy variable has been included for the break in the time deposits series and, consequently, the M2 series representing the change in the definition of savings deposits at end-1977.

[1] Exclusion of the explanatory variables $Y_{bnpm}/M2$ and especially $10^4/M2$ leads to considerably higher estimates of the interest rate effects [cf. Fase (1984)].

Table 2.8
Estimation results for the other coefficients of the portfolio behaviour model for the money stock under the symmetry and zero contraints

	$\dot{p}_{y_{bnpm}}$	r_d	r_{TV}	r_{sc}	$10^4/M2$	$Y_{bnpm} \cdot \alpha_1/M2$
$\Delta CH/M2$	-0.083	0	-0.00083	0	0.41004	0.14828
	(4.72)		(4.72)		(17.82)	(6.45)
$\Delta D/M2$	0.013	0.00816	-0.00833	0.00030	-0.08679	0.42804
	(4.72)	(15.13)	(15.84)	(1.15)	(2.04)	(8.88)
$\Delta TV/M2$	0.066	-0.00834	0.00998	-0.00098	-0.41059	-0.53037
	(4.72)	(15.13)	(11.42)	(1.14)	(9.17)	(10.46)
$\Delta KOS_{ps}/M2$	0.004	0.00018	-0.00082	0.00068	0.08734	-0.04595
	(4.72)	(15.14)	(1.37)	(1.13)	(4.18)	(1.96)
Σ	0	0	0	0	0	0

Table 2.9
Long-term effects in the portfolio behaviour model for the money stock

	coefficients					
	$\dot{p}_{y_{bnpm}}$	r_d	r_{TV}	r_{sc}	$10^4/M2$	$Y_{bnpm} \cdot \alpha_1/M2$
CH/M2	-0.083	0	-0.001	0	0.410	0.148
D/M2	0	0.012	-0.012	0	-0.104	0.687
TV/M2	0.083	-0.012	0.014	-0.002	-0.589	-0.704
$KOS_{ps}/M2$	0	0	-0.002	0.002	0.282	-0.131

* Calculated for the values of the variables in 1982:IV.

	seasonal dummies				
dumb6	d_1	d_2	d_3	constant	standard error of residuals
-0.01629 (8.56)	0.00056 (0.27)	0.00456 (2.21)	-0.00200 (1.17)	0.05144 (2.91)	0.0052
-0.00318 (0.73)	0.02154 (4.86)	0.03963 (8.96)	0.00984 (2.74)	0.14134 (3.82)	0.0118
0.01892 (4.08)	-0.01973 (4.23)	-0.04176 (9.01)	-0.01544 (4.09)	0.72917 (18.78)	0.0125
0.00055 (0.28)	-0.00238 (1.11)	-0.00242 (1.16)	0.00761 (4.34)	0.07805 (4.47)	0.0051
0	0	0	0	1	

elasticities*					
$\dot{p}_{y_{bnpm}}$	r_d	r_{TV}	r_{sc}	$10^4/M2$	$Y_{bnpm} \cdot \alpha_1/M2$
-0.026	0	-0.038	0	0.179	0.586
0	0.042	-0.255	0	-0.021	1.283
0.012	-0.040	0.299	-0.035	-0.117	-1.265
0	0	-0.641	0.604	0.979	-4.090

Both portfolio behaviour models have been estimated with liquid savings, as is customary, being included in time deposits. Re-estimation of the systems with liquid savings as a component of (genuine) savings proved to affect the estimation results barely, if at all. The relevant results are given in the Annex to this Chapter.

2.4.2. *Lending*

The private sector's demand for bank loans is described by two equations. The first explains the demand for short-term loans, BL. The explanatory variables are expected sales SA_{-1}/p_{sa}, the lending rate, r_{bl}, the long-term interest rate, r_l, as an indicator of an alternative source of finance, and investment of enterprises, IB. The demand for loans is assumed to be first-order homogeneous in the price of sales, p_{sa}, while allowance is made for lagged adjustment. Apart from a constant term and seasonal dummy variables, the equation concerned is:

$$\ln BL/p_{sa} = 0.793 \ln (BL/p_{sa})_{-1} + 0.515 \ln (SA_{-1}/p_{sa}) - 0.014 \ln r_{bl} +$$

$$+ 0.039 \ln r_l + 0.0034 \ln (IB/p_{sa})_{-1}$$

On account of the log-linear specification, the coefficients also represent short-term elasticities. The coefficient of adjustment is 0.8. The long-term elasticities of the lending rate and the long-term interest rate are –0.07 and 0.2, respectively, which are low. The long-term sales elasticity is 2.5.

In a major respect, the private sector's demand for long-term loans, LOG_{ps}, has been specified differently from its demand for short-term loans. In conformity with the balance-sheet-oriented structure of the model, BL, as a dependent variable in the demand equation for short-term loans, has been measured as a stock. This stock approach is in line with the short maturities of such loans permitting considerable adjustments of stocks between observations. In the case of long-term loans, changes in stocks can only be very gradual. Consequently, within the framework of a quarterly model, special importance attaches to the explanation of the (net) credit flow. Thus, the equation for the demand for long-term loans determines the change in LOG_{ps}.

The demand for long-term loans consists of various components. It contains demand for mortgage loans, as well as demand of enterprises for private loans, mortgage bonds, bonds and new share capital. The determinants of the demand for long-term loans derive from the principal purposes for which such loans are used by the private sector, viz financing investment (enterprises) and financing dwellings and buildings (households and enterprises), with the long-term interest rate, r_l, as the price of such loans and that of short-term loans, r_k, as opportunity costs. Apart from a constant term and seasonal dummy variables, the equation finally chosen is as follows:

$$\Delta LOG_{ps} = 0.76\ IB - 0.09\ r_l\ .\ IB + 0.02\ r_k\ .\ IB + 0.01\ p_w\ .\ V_w +$$
$$+\ 15{,}642\ (A_q^g)_{-1} - 390\ kr$$

where IB represents investment of enterprises, r_l and r_k the long-term and the short-term interest rate, respectively, $p_w.V_w$ the value of the housing stock, $(A_q^g)_{-1}$ the adjusted labour income ratio and kr a 0–1 variable for the absence or presence of credit restrictions imposed by the Bank.

The above equation has been chosen on the grounds of both the goodness of fit and the economic plausibility of the estimates. The latter is apparent from the values of the elasticities calculated for 1978. For the long-term interest rate, an elasticity was calculated of −1.1, and for the short-term interest rate of 0.2. With regard to the value of the housing stock – which acts as proxy for turnover on the markets for new and existing dwellings – an elasticity of 0.55 was found. The elasticity with regard to the labour income ratio is 1.8. The elasticity with regard to investment of enterprises is about 0.4.

The long-term funds raised by the private sector, LOG_{ps}, are granted by the banking system and the institutional investors. Both supply components are endogenous in the model and are described by an allocation model consisting of two equations. A change in the share of the banks follows from:

$$\Delta(LK_{b,ps}/LOG_{ps}) = 0.19\ \Delta(BTB/BTOT) + 0.0005\ r_k -$$
$$-\ 0.0039\ r_s - 0.0010\ kr$$

The above equation and the identity $LOG_{ps} = LK_{b,ps} + LK_{fs,gb}$ allow derivation of the equation for a change in the share of the institutional investors, $LK_{fs,gb}/LOG_{ps}$. The explanatory factors are the short and the long-term interest rate, the dummy variable kr for the presence or absence of credit restrictions, and the growth of the relative balance sheet total, BTB/BTOT. The last variable represents the growth of the banks' business, BTB, relative to that of all lending institutions, BTOT. Part of the growth of this balance sheet total is determined by exogenous factors, the remainder being the result of the banking system's portfolio investment behaviour. Part of this behaviour consists of the raising of savings deposits, which is represented by an equation describing the banks' share in the market for savings deposits, S_b/S. Apart from seasonal dummy variables and a constant term, the equation is:

$$S_b/S = 0.94\ (S_b/S)_{-1} + 0.001\ (r_s - r_k) + 0.0012\ kr$$

The difference between the interest rate on savings deposits and the short-term interest rate, $(r_s - r_k)$, and the presence or absence of credit restrictions, are the principal determinants in this equation. The need to endogenize this share is, incidentally, solely due to the fact that – by analogy with the demand for long-term loans – the model contains a demand equation for total savings deposits, whereas the balance sheet set-up requires a breakdown by banks and institutional investors.

2.4.3. *External capital transactions*

External capital transactions are described by five behavioural equations relating to different sectors and a number of identities extending across these sectors. A starting-point is offered by the equations for total net foreign assets, NBA. This aggregate is split up into the net foreign assets of the private sector NBA_{ps}, of the banks, NBA_b, and of the government, NBA_o. The last component has, incidentally, been assumed to be exogenous. With regard to the endogenous net foreign assets of the private sector, the following applies:

$$NBA_{ps} = NBA_{ps_{-1}} + \Delta BNIB - \Delta BBIN$$

Private sector holdings of foreign liabilities, BNIB, constitute an asset in the private sector's balance sheet, which is described in the allocation model in section 2.4.1.2 together with the other assets of this sector. Foreign holdings of domestic liabilities, BBIN, constitute a liability in the private sector's balance sheet. In the relevant behavioural equation these holdings, which ensue from both long-term and very short-term capital transactions, are explained from the changes in the long-term interest rate differential against other countries, $\Delta(r_l - r_l^{bu})$, net exports of goods and services, excluding ships and aircraft, $(B_{-sa} - M_{-sa})$, and the increase in long-term government debt, ΔVAS. Additionally, the exchange rate expectation for the Deutsche mark, $\Delta cadm$, plays a role. Apart from a constant term and dummy variables, the equation for foreign holdings of domestic liabilities is:

$$\begin{aligned}\Delta BBIN/MW = {} & 577.17\ \Delta(r_l - r_l^{bu})_{-1/2} - 0.13\ (B_{-sa} - M_{-sa})/MW - \\ & - 0.25\ (B_{-sa} - M_{-sa})_{-1}/MW + 0.11\ \Delta VAS/MW - \\ & - 194.54\ \Delta cadm_{-1/2} \cdot 100\end{aligned}$$

The theoretical basis of this specification is the stock-flow model in the portfolio theory, which considers both reallocations within the existing investment portfolio induced by changes in relative interest rates, and the allocation of new funds on the grounds of interest rate differentials. In this respect, reweighted world imports, MW, act as the scale variable. Similar considerations from the portfolio theory underlie the equation for the net foreign assets of the banks, NBA_b. Apart from a constant term and dummy variables, the equation concerned [which has been derived from Den Butter, Fase and Huijser (1970)] is:

$$NBA_b = 0.80\ NBA_{b_{-1}} - 103\ (r_l - r_l^{bu}) + 0.40\ (B_{-sa} - M_{-sa}) -$$

$$- 0.62\ (SWAP - 0.80\ SWAP_{-1})$$

where the variable SWAP represents the amount of the dollar swaps between the central bank and the banks. As noted before, in the identity

$$NBA = NBA_{ps} + NBA_b + NBA_o$$

the net foreign assets of the government are exogenous. In quantitative terms, this item is, incidentally, of minor significance, as was illustrated in the government's balance sheet as at end-1979.

The next behavioural equations describe the external trade credit received and granted in each period, ΔHKO_{bu} and ΔHKV_{bu}, respectively. Net external trade credit, ΔHK_{bu}, is equal to the difference between the balance on current account on a cash basis and that on a transaction basis. Apart from statistical discrepancies, this is described by the identity

$$LR = E + \Delta HK_{bu}$$

This equation thus provides a link between the variables of the real economic block and the balance sheet changes of the monetary block.

The reaction equations for external trade credit received and granted have, in principle, the same structure. In the equation for trade credit received, the changes in the domestic lending rate, r_{bl}, and the increase in imports of goods and services, excluding ships and aircraft, ΔM_{-sa}, are the principal determinants. The corresponding factors for trade credit granted are the change in the lending rate abroad, Δr_{bl}^{bu}, and the change in exports of goods and services, excluding ships and aircraft, ΔB_{-sa}, respectively. Apart from a constant term and dummy variables these equations are:

$$\Delta HKO_{bu}/M_{-sa_{-1}} = 0.006\ \Delta r_{bl} + 0.053\ \Delta M_{-sa}/M_{-sa_{-1}} + 0.076\ (\Delta M_{-sa}/M_{-sa_{-1}})_{-1}$$

and

$$\Delta HKV_{bu}/B_{-sa_{-1}} = 0.011\ \Delta r_{bl}^{bu} + 0.199\ \Delta B_{-sa}/B_{-sa_{-1}} + 0.107\ (\Delta B_{-sa}/B_{-sa_{-1}})_{-1}$$

2.4.4 Long and short-term interest rates

Any economy is marked by a spectrum of interest rates, while in an open economy such as that of the Netherlands allowance must also be made for interest rates abroad. As a monetary model cannot ignore this situation, the present model distinguishes a number of domestic and foreign interest rates. In principle, an interest rate is the result either of supply of and demand for financial assets or of price setting by the lender or the borrower. Which situation applies to reality depends on the prevailing type of market, where price setting relationships in a sense reflect departures from a situation of full competition towards what is known in market theory as monopoly or monopsony.

The present monetary sub-model comprises six endogenous interest rates. The most important are the short and the long-term interest rate, r_k and r_l, respectively. The other rates are closely connected with the short-term interest rate. The latter is mainly determined by the short-term interest rate in the Federal Republic of Germany, r_k^{DU}, and foreign exchange market conditions, represented here by the spot premium for the Deutsche mark, cadm, and the balance on external goods and services transactions, excluding ships and aircraft ($B_{-sa} - M_{-sa}$). Apart from a constant term and the dummy variable for extremely high short-term interest rates in defence of the guilder, the equation in question is as follows:

$$r_k = 0.99\ r_k^{DU} + 43.27\ \text{cadm} - 33.41\ (B_{-sa} - M_{-sa})_{-1/2}/(B_{-sa} + M_{-sa})$$

As explained below, the endogenous exchange rate variable, cadm, constitutes the link with the Bank's intervention policy in the foreign exchange market, which could influence the exchange rate of the Deutsche mark and exchange rate expectations. The equation for the short-term interest rate can be viewed as a highly stylized description of a number of considerations – such as the obligations ensuing from membership of the European Monetary System (EMS) – underlying the Bank's money and foreign exchange market policy.

Unlike the equation for the short-term interest rate, that for the long-term interest rate reflects the market mechanism, describing the determinants of the movements in the long-term interest rate, r_l. These determinants are the short-term interest rate, r_k, inflationary expectations, $\dot{p}_{y_{bnpm}}$, long-term interest rates abroad, r_l^{DU}, r_l^{VS}, expectations with regard to the dollar's exchange rate, $\hat{e}_\$$, and the tension in the capital market, Sp. Apart from a constant term, the equation is as follows:

$$r_l = 2.19\,\dot{p}_{y_{bnpm}} + 0.10\,r_k + 0.42\,r_l^{DU} + 0.28\,r_l^{VS} + 4.35\,\hat{e}_\$ + 11.04\,Sp$$

The inclusion of the tension variable Sp and the rate of inflation as explanatory variables clearly brings out the nature of this interest rate equation. As was already noted in the outline of the model, this equation combines determinants from the capital market, without specifying the structure of this market explicitly, with influences from the real economic sector. In brief, a sort of reduced form equation.

The tension variable Sp represents:

$$\sum_{j=0}^{3} DVL'_{-j}/\alpha_2 \cdot \sum_{j=0}^{3} Y_{nnpmb_{-j}}$$

where DVL′ is government borrowing and net private sector borrowing in the capital market, and Y_{nnpmb} is disposable national income. The latter quantity acts as the scale variable (α_2 is a correction factor for the 1977 break in series in the National Accounts data and serves a purely arithmetical purpose). In terms of the capital market-related balance sheet items of the various sectors, the following identity holds for DVL′:

$$DVL' = \Delta VAS + \Delta LK_{b,ps} + \Delta LK_{fs,gb} - \Delta LK_{ps,b}$$

or

$$DVL' = \Delta VAS + \Delta LOG_{ps} - \Delta LK_{ps,b}$$

Returning to the equation for the long-term interest rate, it may be noted that the inclusion of the exchange rate expectation variable, $\hat{e}_\$$, means an additional link with the foreign exchange market.

As observed earlier, the other four endogenous interest rates have been linked to the short-term interest rate. As is evident from equation (30), the interest rate on current-account balances, r_d, is explained from the change in the share of these balances in the balance sheet total, $\Delta D/BTB$, and the lagged short-term interest rate, r_k. The interest rate on savings deposits, r_s, likewise follows from the short-term interest rate and the relative growth of savings deposits with money-creating institutions [see equation (31)]. Both equations reflect the relative supply behaviour of the banking system. For empirical reasons, the interest rate on three-month Treasury paper, r_{sc}, has been linked to the short-term interest rate [see equation (32)]. The equation for the interest rate on short-term bank loans, r_{bl}, is also a price setting relationship, with the lending rate being traditionally tied to the discount rate on promissory notes, r_{cb}. Additionally, allowance has been made for a variable surcharge where prompted by the movements in money market rates. This has been done in the relevant periods by adding a dummy variable, $dumr_{bl}$, to the difference between the short-term interest rate and the official discount rate, $(r_k - r_{cb})$, and to the banking system's scope for lending, $\Delta BL/BTB$, respectively. Apart from the remaining dummy variables and a constant term, the equation for the interest rate on short-term bank loans is:

$$r_{bl} = r_{cb} + 0.33\ dumr_{bl}\ (r_k - r_{cb}) + 0.23\ (dumr_{bl}\ (r_k - r_{cb}))_{-1} +$$

$$+ 18.73\ dumr_{bl}\ (\Delta BL/BTB)_{-1}$$

Finally, the sub-model incorporates two identities for the interest rate on time deposits, r_{TV}, and the interest rate on the money stock, r_{M2}. These are self-evident [see equations (34) and (35)].

2.4.5 Foreign exchange market

In the present model the exchange rate of the dollar, expectations as to the dollar rate, and the exchange rate of the Deutsche mark are assumed to be endogenous. The foreign exchange market block consists of five equations, viz (36) to (40).

The key equation in this exchange rate block describes the relative change in the dollar's exchange rate in terms of guilders, $\dot{e}_{\$}$. On account of the obligations ensuing from EMS membership, the principal determinant is the rate of the dollar against the Deutsche mark, $\dot{e}_{DM.\$}$, which is assumed to be exogenous. Consequently, the volume of the Bank's interventions in the foreign exchange market, ΔNBA_{cb}, has also been included as a determinant. For the central bank this is a policy variable. Besides, changes in money market rates at home and abroad, r_k and r_k^{DU}, differences in rates of inflation, $\dot{p}_{VS} - \dot{p}_{DU}$, and the balance on external goods and services transactions, excluding ships and aircraft, play a role as explanatory variables. Apart from a dummy variable and a constant term, the relevant equation is:

$$\dot{e}_{\$} = 20\ \Delta\Delta NBA_{cb}/(B_{-sa} + M_{-sa}) - 0.35\ \Delta r_k + 0.92\ \Delta r_k^{DU} +$$

$$+ 0.22\ \Delta r_k^{VS} + 0.85\ \dot{e}_{DM.\$} - 0.32\ (\dot{p}_{VS} - \dot{p}_{DU}) -$$

$$- 20.37\ \Delta(B_{-sa} - M_{-sa})/(B_{-sa} + M_{-sa})$$

The volume of the foreign exchange market interventions is defined by distinguishing not only the endogenous change in the holdings of gold and foreign exchange, ΔIR, but also an autonomous change, ΔIR_{aut}. This ensures the model's internal consistency. The equation for the foreign exchange market intervention thus defined is as follows:

$$\Delta NBA_{cb} = \Delta IR - \Delta IR_{aut}$$

The exchange rate expectations for the dollar in terms of guilders are described here by a linear distributed lag of recent exchange rates. This equation is very simple:

$$\hat{\dot{e}}_{\$} = 0.50\ \dot{e}_{\$} + 0.25\ \dot{e}_{\$_{-1}} + 0.15\ \dot{e}_{\$_{-2}} + 0.10\ \dot{e}_{\$_{-3}}$$

The remaining exchange rate equations are identities. Equation (39) defines the changes in the cross exchange rate, equation (40) the spot premium of the Deutsche mark.

The complete monetary sub-model, including a number of statistics, is given in Appendix I, equations (1) to (52).

2.5 Residual items

The design of a monetary model within the framework of a coherent system of balance sheets implies that a number of balance sheet items is determined by the equality of assets and liabilities in these balance sheets (see Table 2.2). As noted by Brainard and Tobin (1968), these residual items are the mirror image of those balance sheet items which are either described in behavioural equations or are assumed to be exogenous. The equations for the residual items follow implicitly from the explicitly formulated relationships. These implicit behavioural relationships have as a characteristic that their justification in economic theory is much less definite. This is, incidentally, unavoidable, being an inescapable consequence of the logic of the system chosen, which leaves no degrees of freedom for the residual items.

In the private sector's balance sheet, the portfolio model causes the total supply of financial assets to be allocated among the various components of demand. Consequently, this balance sheet does not include any explicit residual item.

In the balance sheet of the money-creating institutions, the borrowed reserves, GLR, follow as a residual item from the balance sheet equality. This means that borrowed reserves follow indirectly from the central bank's policy, the net foreign assets and the price setting behaviour of the banking system.

In the government's balance sheet, the Treasury's balance, SSCH, is the residual item. This is fully in accordance with the buffer function usually performed by this balance in reality.

Finally, the gold and foreign exchange holdings follow as a residual item from the balance of payments, although it is possible to argue with equal justification that this item is the residual item in the central bank's balance sheet. However, as noted earlier, the central bank's balance sheet equality was already ensured implicitly by the equality of the other balance sheets (see Table 2.2). This aspect of the model's structure illustrates the way in which the model describes the central bank's behaviour with regard to the holdings of gold and foreign exchange. This description is, however, indirect and proceeds via the banks' net foreign assets and interest rates, which in turn influence the private sector's capital transactions.

To conclude and illustrate the foregoing, the implicit behavioural equation for the borrowed reserves is derived below by means of substitution of the other items forming part of the banks' balance sheet equality. In this balance sheet equality, written for GLR:

$$GLR = VR + NBA_b + BL + KOS_b + LK_b + DA_b - D - TV - S_b - \\ - LK_{ps,b} - KT_{ro} - V_b$$

VR, DA_b, KT_{ro} and V_b are exogenous. For all other items, the model comprises behavioural equations. Consequently, the determinants in these equations affect GLR. In the first round, substitution produces the following relationship:

$$GLR = f(B_{-sa} - M_{-sa}, SWAP, p_{sa}, r_{bl}, r_l, FT^*_o, p_{y_{bnpm}}, \\ Y_{bnpm}, r_d, r_{sc}, r_{M2}, r_k, r_{TV}, r_s, r_l^{bu}, cadm, q_k, \\ MW, BTB/BTOT, kr, IB, p_w \cdot V_w, VAS)$$

A number of the determinants included in the above relationship is, in turn, dependent on other monetary variables via a behavioural equation. This example shows the complex behavioural relationship which, in principle, underlies this residual item. However, the above equation also shows that the instruments of the central bank and the interest rate variables used by the banking system, via price setting, to influence its portfolio composition are among the many determinants of this residual item. Additionally, developments in the real economic sector and developments in the rest of the world play a role as well.

This example also illustrates a distinct drawback of the residual item system in that the formulation of the model's behavioural equations must already make allowance for the choice of the model's residual item. Secondly, the choice of the model's residual item is, in a sense, fairly arbitrary. It might, for instance, be argued that in the banking system's balance sheet the net foreign assets would be more eligible to serve as the residual item than the borrowed reserves. In a sense, this is the price which must be paid for the model's consistency.

Annex to Chapter 2

Allocation models not distinguishing between genuine and liquid savings

In the Bank's monetary analysis, a so-called virulent part of savings deposits held with money-creating institutions is counted, on the basis of the movements in the accounts concerned, as liquid assets [cf. e.g. Van Straaten (1981)]. The question arises to what extent the empirical estimations for the portfolio models, which include this distinction between genuine and liquid savings, have been affected by this typical characteristic. In order to answer this question, the analysis presented in sections 2.4.1.2 and 2.4.1.3 has been repeated, no distinction being made between liquid and other savings deposits. In line with the above sections, the results are given in Tables 2.4A to 2.9A. Comparison with the corresponding Tables in sections 2.4.1.2 and 2.4.1.3 shows that in most cases the differences are very minor. The most striking difference is the virtual absence of a cyclical effect on the money stock excluding liquid savings, M2′.

It will be clear that this analysis has no consequences for the distinction between genuine and liquid savings. That distinction is largely a matter of monetary policy design, which – in line with the balance sheet set-up – acts upon the assets and the liabilities side of the money-creating institutions' balance sheet (in this case the money-creating operations), whereas the key policy variable – the money stock – relates to the private sector's liquid assets.

Table 2.5A
Estimation results for the other coefficients of the portfolio behaviour model for financial assets under the symmetry and zero constraints (M2 excluding liquid savings)

	$r_{M2'}$	r_s	r_l	r_l^{bu}	$Y_{bnpm} \cdot \alpha_1/FA$	$\Delta cadm$
$\Delta M2'/FA$	0.002503 (6.13)	-0.001142 (6.07)	0.000231 (0.63)	-0.001593 (3.96)	0.30265 (9.17)	-0.01132 (0.37)
$\Delta S'/FA$	-0.001996 (6.09)	0.001997 (6.09)	-0.001709 (3.97)	0.001709 (3.97)	0.11507 (2.77)	0.02491 (0.83)
$\Delta LK_{ps}/FA$	-0.000418 (2.20)	-0.000392 (6.13)	0.001808 (5.63)	-0.000998 (3.96)	-0.37563 (12.83)	-0.04068 (1.91)
$\Delta BNIB/FA$	-0.000089 (6.50)	-0.000463 (6.09)	-0.000330 (1.29)	0.000882 (3.96)	-0.04209 (2.03)	0.02709 (2.06)
Σ	0	0	0	0	0	0

Table 2.4A
Estimation results for the coefficients of adjustment in the portfolio behaviour model for financial assets (M2 excluding liquid savings)

	$M2'_{-1}$/FA	S'_{-1}/FA	$LK_{ps_{-1}}$/FA	$BNIB_{-1}$/FA
ΔM2'/FA	-0.8545	-0.6602	-0.3840	0
	(19.38)	(11.50)	(5.86)	
ΔS'/FA	0	-0.3398	0	-0.4120
		(5.92)		(3.45)
ΔLK_{ps}/FA	-0.0667	0	-0.3465	-0.1059
	(1.55)		(5.22)	(0.81)
ΔBNIB/FA	-0.0788	0	-0.2695	-0.4821
	(2.97)		(6.08)	(5.72)
Σ	-1	-1	-1	-1

	q_k	ΔBBIN/FA	dumb6	seasonal dummies d_1	d_2	d_3	constant	standard error of residuals
ΔM2'/FA	0.03367	-0.32943	0.00421	0.00723	0.00825	0.00472	0.39405	0.0032
	(4.51)	(2.73)	(3.79)	(8.41)	(9.07)	(5.55)	(59.80)	
ΔS'/FA	-0.03644	-0.11515	-0.00624	0.00139	0.00003	0.00032	0.14820	0.0031
	(5.55)	(0.97)	(4.69)	(1.64)	(0.03)	(0.38)	(30.62)	
ΔLK_{ps}/FA	0.02145	0.29011	0.00203	-0.00466	0.00470	0.00389	0.22606	0.0023
	(3.36)	(3.43)	(2.18)	(7.52)	(7.23)	(6.48)	(46.32)	
ΔBNIB/FA	-0.01868	0.15447	0.00000	-0.00396	0.00358	0.00115	0.23169	0.0015
	(5.22)	(2.90)	(0.01)	(10.42)	(8.95)	(3.11)	(77.49)	
Σ	0	0	0	0	0	0	1	

Table 2.6A
Long-term effects in the portfolio behaviour model for financial assets (M2 excluding liquid savings)

	coefficients					
	$r_{M2'}$	r_s	r_l	r_l^{bu}	$Y_{bnpm} \cdot \alpha_1 / FA$	q_k
M2′/FA	0.0088	-0.0059	-0.0029	0	1.27	-0.001
S′/FA	-0.0059	0.0059	0	0	-0.32	0
LK_{ps}/FA	-0.0029	0	0.0070	-0.0042	-1.49	0.089
BNIB/FA	0	0	-0.0042	0.0042	0.54	-0.088

* Calculated for the values of the variables in 1982:IV.

Table 2.7A
Estimation results for the coefficients of adjustment in the portfolio behaviour model for the money stock (M2 excluding liquid savings)

	CH_{-1}/M2′	D_{-1}/M2′	TV'_{-1}/M2′	$KOS_{ps_{-1}}$/M2′
ΔCH/M2′	-1	0	0	0
ΔD/M2′	0	-0.83948 (8.86)	-0.14062 (4.03)	-0.31784 (1.39)
ΔTV′/M2′	0	-0.09210 (0.96)	-0.8	-0.24605 (1.03)
ΔKOS_{ps}/M2′	0	-0.06842 (1.33)	-0.05938 (1.70)	-0.43612 (3.80)
Σ	-1	-1	-1	-1

elasticities*					
$r_{M2'}$	r_s	r_l	r_l^{bu}	$Y_{bnpm} \cdot \alpha_1 / FA$	q_k
0.23	−0.22	−0.15	0	0.95	−0.003
−0.13	0.19	0	0	−0.20	0
−0.03	0	0.14	−0.09	−0.41	0.16
0	0	−0.23	0.25	0.42	−0.45

Table 2.8A
Estimation results for the other coefficients of the portfolio behaviour model for the money stock (excluding liquid savings) under the symmetry and zero constraints

	$\dot{p}_{y_{bnpm}}$	r_d	r_{TV}	r_{sc}	$10^4/M2'$	$Y_{bnpm} \cdot \alpha_1/M2'$
$\Delta CH/M2'$	-0.084 (4.20)	0	-0.00083 (4.72)	0	0.41070 (20.43)	0.14623 (6.41)
$\Delta D/M2'$	0.012 (4.20)	0.00832 (16.64)	-0.00857 (17.14)	0.00036 (1.20)	-0.08734 (2.07)	0.44974 (9.47)
$\Delta TV'/M2'$	0.067 (4.20)	-0.00843 (16.64)	0.01023 (11.37)	-0.00113 (1.26)	-0.40567 (9.10)	-0.54219 (10.76)
$\Delta KOS_{ps}/M2'$	0.005 (4.20)	0.00011 (16.64)	-0.00082 (1.37)	0.00077 (1.28)	0.08231 (3.98)	-0.05378 (2.29)
Σ	0	0	0	0	0	0

Table 2.9A
Long-term effects in the portfolio behaviour model for the money stock (excluding liquid savings)

	coefficients					
	$\dot{p}_{y_{bnpm}}$	r_d	r_{TV}	r_{sc}	$10^4/M2'$	$Y_{bnpm} \cdot \alpha_1/M2'$
$CH/M2'$	-0.084	0	-0.001	0	0.411	0.146
$D/M2'$	0	0.012	-0.012	0	-0.115	0.708
$TV'/M2'$	0.084	-0.012	0.015	-0.002	-0.582	-0.717
$KOS_{ps}/M2'$	0	0	-0.002	0.002	0.285	-0.137

* Calculated for the values of the variables in 1982:IV.

	seasonal dummies				
dumb6	d_1	d_2	d_3	constant	standard error of residuals
−0.01667 (8.77)	0.00043 (0.20)	0.00449 (2.14)	−0.00214 (1.26)	0.05395 (3.03)	0.005
−0.00260 (0.73)	0.02345 (4.86)	0.04173 (8.96)	0.01057 (2.74)	0.11660 (3.82)	0.012
−0.01858 (3.95)	−0.02050 (4.36)	−0.04296 (9.14)	−0.00158 (4.16)	0.73567 (18.82)	0.013
0.00069 (0.35)	−0.00338 (1.54)	−0.00326 (1.48)	0.00737 (4.09)	0.09378 (5.33)	0.005
0	0	0	0	1	

elasticities*					
$\dot{p}_{y_{bnpm}}$	r_d	r_{TV}	r_{sc}	$10^4/M2'$	$Y_{bnpm} \cdot \alpha_1/M2'$
−0.026	0	−0.038	0	0.180	0.578
0	0.042	−0.253	0	−0.024	1.323
0.012	−0.041	0.312	−0.040	−0.120	−1.332
0	0	−0.725	0.685	0.992	−4.281

3 The relationships in the real economic sector

3.1 Income and expenditure

As a consistent set of balance sheets provides the framework for the monetary sector, so a confrontation of income and expenditure, in principle, provides the framework for the real economic sector. Using the symbols of the sub-model of the real economic sector, Table 3.1 shows this confrontation (in billions of guilders) for the fourth quarter of 1979.

Table 3.1
Confrontation of income and expenditure
(current prices, billions of guilders; fourth quarter 1979)

Income			Expenditure		
Output Y_{bnpm}:			Consumption:		
– Enterprises Y_{bm}	72.1		– Private sector C	51.2	
– Government Y_{ov}	11.3		– Government X′	14.6	
– Foreign sector ($B_p - M_p$)	0.4				
					65.8
		83.8	Investment of enterprises:		
			– Dwellings I_{wo}	5.4	
			– Other fixed assets ($I - I_{wo}$)	10.4	
			– Stockbuilding N	-0.4	
			Government X′	2.9	
					18.3
Imports M		47.1	Exports B		46.8
Total income		130.9	Total expenditure		130.9

It goes without saying that this confrontation only gives a broad picture. Nevertheless it contains the basics of the model of the real economic sector. Elaboration concerns first of all a distinction by volume and value, endogenizing the determination of prices. Furthermore, the above confrontation reflects the employment of the factors of production and their prices, which are to be explained by the model. The concrete elaboration, viz in behavioural and other reaction equations and identities, is discussed in the sections below.

3.2 The real economic model in outline

The sub-model for the real economic sector contains 90 equations, including 17 behavioural equations which have been statistically estimated with seasonally unadjusted quarterly data for the period 1970:I-1979:IV. In connection with this, seasonal dummies were included throughout in the estimation equations, insofar as applicable. The real economic part of the complete model is also included in Appendix I [notably equations (53) to (142)].

The sub-model for the real economic sector is not only demand-determined, but also pays attention to the supply side, as is reflected in output, with stockbuilding as the difference between output and demand, investment and the labour supply. For the description of this sub-model a distinction is made into six categories with interrelated behavioural equations. These categories, which are in line with those used by the Bank in its Annual Reports, are:

. Domestic expenditure
. Goods trade with the rest of the world
. Labour market and wage determination
. Output
. Price determination
. Income distribution and the public sector

The next section gives a brief description of the relevant behavioural equations per category.

The econometric model for the real economic sector is a simultaneous one. This means that the endogeneous economic variables of this sub-model influence each other. An outline of these interactions is shown in Chart 3.1, which represents the essence of the real economic sector. This flow diagram gives a first, overall impression, analogous to the diagram for the monetary sector (cf. Chart 2.1). Here, too, black arrows indicate the influence within the real economic submodel. The broken arrows show the influence emanating from the monetary sector, the rest of the world and policy. The diagram indicates that policy affects notably expenditure, the government's financial balance and the distribution of income. Especially expenditure is influenced by monetary factors. The diagram shows that the monetary sector, which is exogenous for the real economic sector, feels a substantial impact of the current account, domestic expenditure and the government's financial balance. This reflects the fact that the link between the monetary and the real economic sector runs via the macro-economic budget equation. Expenditure influences the financial balance of the government both directly and via the demand for labour. The utilization rate of

Chart 3.1
Flow diagram of the real economic block of MORKMON

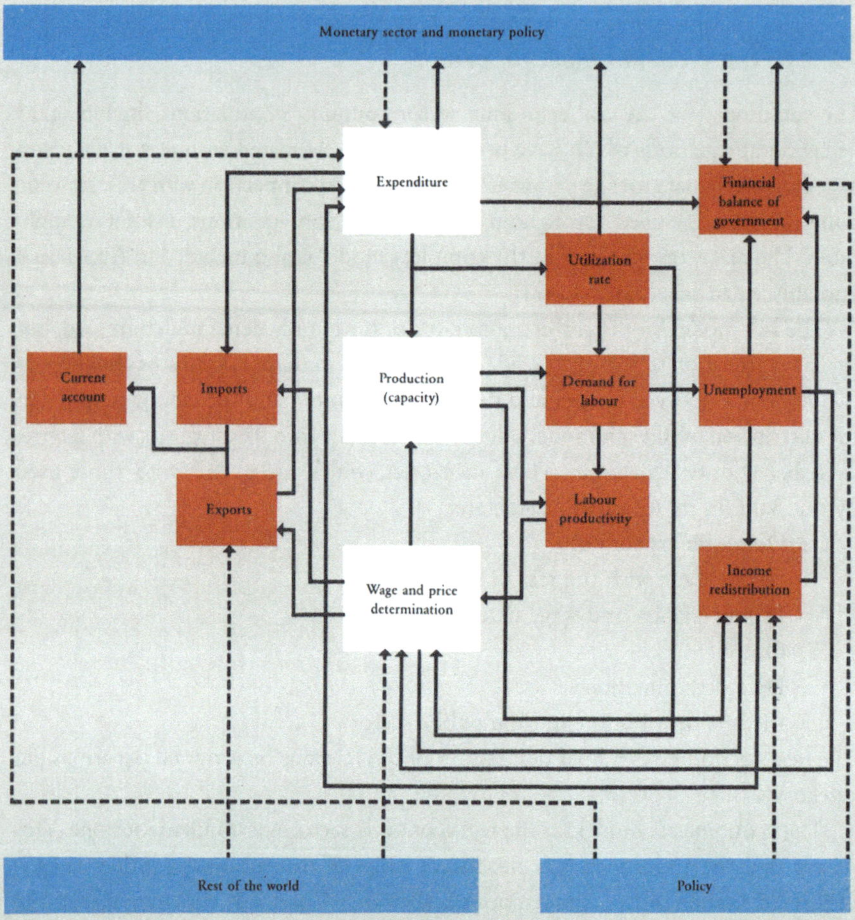

capital is, as it were, the indicator for the disequilibrium between expenditure and production (capacity), but also affects imports and exports via wage and price determination, and thus the balance on current account. A flow diagram aims only to give a first impression, within the model used, of both the endogenous relations and the influence of exogenous factors. It does not provide detailed information. For that, the individual equations of the real economic model must be considered. The classification given earlier will be used to that end.

3.3 The behavioural equations of the real economic sector

3.3.1 Domestic expenditure

The model distinguishes three categories of domestic expenditure: private consumption, c, other gross fixed investment of enterprises, excluding ships and aircraft, i_{-sa}, and investment in dwellings, i_{wo}. The quantities considered are expressed in terms of volume.

Consumption at constant prices is calculated from disposable wage and transfer income (including wages imputed to the self-employed), W_d, disposable other income, Z_{od}, the long-term interest rate, r_l, the private sector's net wealth, V_{ps}, and the expected rise in consumer prices, measured as $\dot{p}_{c_{-1}}$. The long-term interest rate reflects the opportunity costs. The expected rate of inflation is included, on the one hand, because of the possible occurrence of money illusion, and, on the other, to evade the arbitrary determination of the real long-term interest rate as the determinant of consumer spending. Finally, a wealth variable has been included in order not to preclude a possible influence on expenditure by wealth as is often postulated in the theory. The explanatory variables have also been deflated with the price index of private consumption, p_c. Apart from a constant term and dummy variables, the following consumption equation has been found:

$$c = 0.84 \sum_{j=0}^{1} \zeta_j (W_d/p_c)_{-j} + 0.29 \sum_{j=0}^{3} \eta_j (Z_{od}/p_c)_{-j} - 116.08\, r_l +$$

$$+ 0.05\, V_{ps}/p_c + 105.93\, \dot{p}_{c_{-1}}$$

The estimations imply a consumption elasticity with regard to wage and transfer income of 0.87. As expected, there is a considerably lower income elasticity in respect of other income, viz 0.04. The interest rate elasticity comes out at –0.3 per percentage point, which, be it with opposite sign, virtually equals the inflation elasticity. The wealth elasticity amounts to 0.16.

Gross other fixed investment of enterprises (excluding ships and aircraft), i_{-sa}, is calculated from the long-term interest rate, r_l, the real value of gross disposable other income, $(Z_{od}/p_{y_{bm}} + f_b)$, and two monetary tension variables, viz the liquidity ratio deviating from its trend, $(LQ - \overline{LQ})$, and the recourse to external financing, $(BL + LOG_{ps})$. Finally, the utilization rate of capital, q_k, acts as an explanatory variable. Apart from a constant term and dummy variables, the estimated equation is as follows:

$$i_{-sa} = 0.29\, i_{-sa_{-1}} - 15.35\,(1/4 \sum_{j=0}^{3} r_{l_{-j}}^{2}) + 0.33\,(1/4 \sum_{j=2}^{5} (Z_{od}/p_{y_{bm}} + f_b)_{-j}) +$$

$$+ 11{,}658.39\,(1/4 \sum_{j=0}^{3} (LQ - 1/8 \sum_{i=0}^{7} LQ_{-i})_{-j}) -$$

$$- 728.69\,(BL + LOG_{ps})/Y_{nnpm} + 2{,}959.10\, q_k$$

In this investment equation the nominal long-term interest rate has been included quadratically, after a number of alternative specifications were tried. The influence of the interest rate consequently increases with its height. In addition, a price variable has been tried as an explanatory variable to approximate the real interest rate, which is often regarded as the determinant of investment. This effort did not yield plausible estimation results.

Investment in dwellings is explained by net national income, y_{nnim}, the long-term interest rate, r_l, and the number of effective hours worked per construction worker, h_{pb}. This behavioural equation thus contains both supply and demand elements. Apart from a constant term and dummy variables, the estimated equation is:

$$i_{wo} = 0.48\, i_{wo_{-1}} + 0.04\,(1/4 \sum_{j=0}^{3} y_{nnim_{-j}}) - 155.30\,(1/2 \sum_{j=0}^{1} r_{l_{-j}}) + 2.0\, h_{pb}$$

Measured at the end of the estimation period, this equation implies a long-term elasticity for the long-term interest rate of –0.70, while for the number of effective hours worked and national income elasticities of 0.8 and 1.3 were found.

3.3.2 Goods trade with the rest of the world

External trade has been modelled by means of an export and an import equation; on account of their often non-recurrent nature and erratic movements, imports and exports of ships, aircraft, oil and gas have been left out of consideration. Imports and exports of services have also been assumed to be exogenous. Again, the variables are expressed in terms of volume.

For the volume of exports of goods, b_{-saog}, a simple log-linear specification has been assumed, implying constant elasticities. The principal determinant of exports is reweighted world trade, m_w. Another factor is the ratio of Dutch export prices to those of competitor countries, $p_{b_{-saog}}/p_{bf}$. It is obvious that relative price differences take time to influence exports. To allow for this, a Koyck lag has been introduced. Finally, an attempt was made to include the utilization rate of capital as an explanatory variable, but this attempt was not successful.

Apart from a constant term and seasonal fluctuations – represented here by an MA process for the disturbances – the estimated equation is as follows:

$$\ln b_{-saog} = 0.72 \ln b_{-saog_{-1}} - 0.34 \ln (p_{b_{-saog}}/p_{bf}) + $$
$$+ 0.98 \ln m_w - 0.70 \ln m_{w_{-1}}$$

The estimation results suggest an almost proportional relationship between world trade and exports, any change in world trade having an immediate effect. Such proportionality is in line with the findings of others in export equations for the Netherlands. Having a long-term value of −1.2, the price substitution elasticity is rather small compared with other empirical results for the Netherlands. The average adjustment lag for this variable is slightly less than four quarters.

For the volume of imports of goods, m_{-saog}, a log-linear specification with a Koyck lag has likewise been assumed. Total expenditure, v, is the principal determinant; moreover, stockbuilding, n, the ratio of the mean import price to that of expenditure, $p_{m_{-saog}}/p_v$, and the utilization rate of capital, q_k, have been included as explanatory variables. Apart from a constant term, seasonal dummy variables and the adjustment for the 1977 revision of the National Accounts, the estimation result is as follows:

$$\ln m_{-saog} = 0.6 \ln m_{-saog_{-1}} - 0.30 \ln (p_{m_{-saog}}/p_v) + $$
$$+ 0.99 (\ln v - 0.6 \ln v_{-1}) + 0.02 (n - 0.6\, n_{-1}) + $$
$$+ 0.42 \ln q_{k_{-1}}$$

In this equation, the average adjustment lag has been set at 2½ quarters. However, the movements in expenditure and stockbuilding are assumed to have an immediate effect on imports; therefore, these variables have been excluded from the Koyck lag. In conformity with most other empirical macro-economic models for the Netherlands, the expenditure elasticity is practically equal to one. The estimation result implies a value for the import ratio of stockbuilding of around 0.5. The absolute value of the long-term price substitution elasticity is higher than one. Moreover, imports are influenced by the utilization rate of capital in such a way that an increase in the utilization rate leads to an increase in imports. This tension variable describes the situation, sometimes topical in times of cyclical upswing, where the home pressure of demand induces purchases abroad on account of more favourable conditions of delivery.

3.3.3 Labour market and wage determination

The block which describes the labour market and wage determination in MORKMON covers both the supply and the demand side of the labour market. On account of the close relationship of the resulting employment with the creation of new jobs, this segment of MORKMON also includes equations for technical relationships associated with production capacity. On the analogy of the procedure used in section 2.4.1, some theoretical considerations are set forth below, after which the empirically estimated relationships are presented.

3.3.3.1 Demand for labour

A characteristic feature of the theoretical sub-model used here for the demand for labour [see equations (59) to (64)] is its departure from the tradition to make the demand for labour dependent upon a vintage model – or within this context – a quarterly equivalent of such a model. The first consideration underlying this departure was the fact that it does not appear reasonable to make the present demand for labour dependent on occasional fluctuations in investment 40 or more quarters ago. Moreover, from the point of view of estimation, this approach would require a much longer observation period than is compatible with the aim of basing the model as much as possible on recent observations. Nevertheless, the present sub-model does contain some elements of the vintage concept as incorporated in the models of the Dutch Central Planning Bureau. The principal differences compared with these models are that the present model makes no explicit distinction between technical and economic obsolescence and that technical progress is non-incorporated. The principal reason is that a vintage-model approach is less suitable in a quarterly model designed for the short term than it is in a model designed primarily to describe medium-term developments.

The sub-model used here for the demand for labour consists of a description of the real stock of capital goods, the determination of production capacity, the determination of the number of jobs and actual employment.

The real stock of capital goods, k, is determined as follows:

$$k = k_{-1} + i_{-sa} - k_a$$

In this equation, the stock of capital goods, k, is equal to the stock of capital goods in the preceding quarter plus investment, i_{-sa}, less scrappage, k_a, in the current quarter. The scrappage of economically and/or technically obsolete capital goods is calculated by means of an equation which, apart from dummy variables, is as follows:

$$k_a = \alpha_0 \, [1 + \alpha_1 \, ((\tfrac{1}{4} \sum_{j=0}^{3} (\dot{\iota}_b^g - \dot{p}_{y_{bm}})_{-j}) - \mu) \, \frac{1}{\mu}] \, k_{-1}$$

In this equation, α_0 is the average scrappage perunage. The term in square brackets denotes the factor by which the actual scrappage perunage differs from the average one if the annual increase in real labour costs, $(\dot{\iota}_b^g - \dot{p}_{y_{bm}})$, differs from technical progress, μ. This ensures the incorporation of the mechanism by which moderation of wage costs has a favourable effect on employment through decreased scrappage of capital goods. However, by contrast with the models of the Dutch Central Planning Bureau, this scrappage does not concern the oldest and least efficient capital goods, but relates to the total stock of capital goods. In addition, the magnitude of the wage cost effect is determined empirically by means of coefficient α_1.

The calculation of production capacity, y^*_{bm}, is symbolized by the following equation:

$$y^*_{bm} = \frac{1}{\varkappa} \cdot k$$

The capital output ratio $\varkappa$ is determined empirically by means of the trend-through-peaks method[1]. Hence, the capital output ratio has not been assumed to be constant.

[1] The trend-through-peaks method takes the peaks in a time series of output figures to be an approximation of available production capacity. This serves to derive the capital output ratio.

In MORKMON the utilization rate of capital, q_k, plays a role as a cyclical tension variable. For this rate, the following identity holds:

$$q_k = y_{bm}/y^*_{bm}$$

where y_{bm} represents actual output of enterprises and y^*_{bm} production capacity or potential output.

As the demand-for-labour block contains a kind of vintage-model approach, both the demand for labour and production capacity follow from it as endogenous variables. This means that the utilization rate of capital and the utilization rate of labour are not directly interrelated as tension variables. Such a model structure would appear to be logical to describe a period which is no longer marked by nearly full employment and in which cyclical tension with regard to production capacity need not necessarily lead to tensions in the labour market.

The number of jobs, a*, follows from:

$$a^* = \phi_0 \,[1 + \phi_1 \,(1 - \frac{h}{h_0})\,]\; k \,.\, e^{-\phi_2 \sum_{j=0}^{t} \mu_j/100}$$

This equation states that, in principle, the number of jobs is proportional to the stock of capital goods. Here, the coefficient ϕ_0 represents the reciprocal of capital costs per job. Additionally, this equation allows for the possibility of a reduction in working time, measured by working time relative to 1970, h/h_0. The formulation means that more jobs become available per unit of capital as working time is reduced. If and to the extent that a reduction in working time is not fully converted into new jobs, coefficient ϕ_1 will be smaller than one. Finally, the equation includes the consequences of technical progress. By contrast with the models of the Dutch Central Planning Bureau, in which technical progress is largely linked to the vintages, the present model assumes non-incorporated technical progress [see e.g. Allen (1968, pp. 237 ff)]. Such technical progress is labour-saving, meaning that the same size of the stock of capital goods involves ever fewer jobs.

Finally, the sub-model for the demand for labour contains an equation representing the relationship between the number of jobs, a*, and actual employment, a. Apart from dummy variables, this equation is as follows:

$$a = a^* - \pi_1 \,[1 - \tfrac{1}{4} \sum_{j=0}^{3} (y_{bm}/y^*_{bm})_{-j}\,]\; a^*$$

It equates employment with the number of jobs less a certain fraction, π_1, of the number of jobs which are redundant owing to underutilization of capacity, represented by y_{bm}/y^*_{bm}. Because of labour market inflexibility, social legislation, etc., not all redundant jobs are shed in a situation of underutilization of capacity. Therefore, coefficient π_1 will be smaller than one. In addition, the equation also comprises the seasonal effects on the demand for labour. Like other dummy variables, they will not be discussed here.

The manner of estimation of the above six technical or behavioural equations differs from the usual method and thus deserves special discussion. In principle, the parameters of the equations have been obtained by minimizing the sum of squares of the calculated less the actual demand for labour. This leads to a non-linear minimization problem. As the capital output ratio $\varkappa$ is derived from the trend-through-peaks method, the sum of squares shows discontinuities and the minimization of this sum cannot be regarded as maximization of the likelihood. Consequently, it is not possible to calculate confidence intervals for the parameter estimates. Additionally, unrestricted estimation does not lead to a unique minimum; for various initial values various (local) minimums are obtained. Moreover, in the case of unrestricted estimation, not all coefficients acquire plausible values. Hence, for a number of coefficients, plausible parameter values have been established in a way other than estimation. Firstly, this concerns the percentage of technical progress, μ, which has been measured on the basis of the actual trend of labour productivity. Secondly, upon free estimation, the value of α_0 becomes so high as to lead to an unacceptably short service life of capital goods. Setting this coefficient at 0.015 not only results in a plausible service life of 16⅔ years [for average periods of installation of capital goods in a number of countries, see Blades (1983)] but it also yields realistic values for the other parameters.

Ultimately, the following coefficients were chosen (° denotes that the value has not been obtained by free estimation):

μ : decreasing from 1.73 %° in 1970:I to 0.94 %° in 1972:I, subsequently 0.94 %° (= 4 % on an annual basis)

$\alpha_0 = 0.015°$	$\phi_0 = 0.0188$	$\phi_2 = 1.170$
$\alpha_1 = 0.373$	$\phi_1 = 0.528$	$\pi_1 = 0.454$

Moreover, in the demand for labour, allowance is made for autocorrelation of the residuals ($\hat{\varrho} = 0.60$).

Generally, the coefficients chosen correspond closely to the results of other studies of the demand-for-labour/output block for the Netherlands. The measured value of coefficient α_1 means that wage costs have such an effect on scrappage of capital goods that, if real wage costs decrease by 1½ % per quarter (or 6 % per annum), no more capital goods are scrapped. In a vintage model, this situation would be aptly described as the maximum extension of service life: the life of the oldest vintage increases every year by one year. The value of coefficient ϕ_0 indicates that in the base year (in this instance 1970) the capital costs of one job are over Fl. 50,000 (1977 prices).

3.3.3.2 Supply of labour

The supply of labour, a_a, which is described by equation (65), is explained by the exogenously determined working-age population, a_p, and unemployment, U, defined by equation (137) as:

$$U = a_a - a_l - a_z - a_{ov}$$

In the labour supply equation, U represents the so-called discouraged-worker effect, i.e. the discouraging effect on newcomers to the labour market exerted by the level of unemployment. Notably the last few years of the observation period have witnessed young people delaying their entry into the labour market by extending their education. This has been reflected in a falling trend in the youth participation rate. To allow for this effect on the labour supply, this participation rate, dnpj, which is assumed to be exogenous to the model, has been included in the equation as an extra explanatory variable, in addition to unemployment. An influence of the income effect on the supply of labour could not be found.

In the estimation of the labour supply equation, allowance was made for the effect of the 1977 revision of the National Accounts and a second-order autocorrelation in the disturbances. Apart from this autocorrelation, a constant term and dummy variables, the estimation result is:

$$a_a = 0.41\, a_p - 0.31\, (\tfrac{1}{4} \sum_{j=1}^{4} U_{-j}) + 50.39\, \text{dnpj}$$

This implies that the marginal ratio of the supply of labour to the working-age population is 0.41, with an average participation rate of the working-age population of 0.56. The discouraged-worker effect is over 0.3 per unemployed person.

3.3.3.3 Wage determination

For the sake of simplicity, only two general categories are distinguished with regard to wage determination: enterprises and government. Wage determination in enterprises and the timing of wage adjustments are to a considerable extent dependent on institutional factors. Yet it is customary in macro-economic models to explain wages by means of a behavioural equation. The usual determinants, in line with the theoretical literature on the subject, are prices, labour productivity and cyclical tension. The present wage equation has been specified along these lines, with the wage and salary bill per worker in enterprises, l_b^g, as the dependent variable, and the consumption price index transformed into a so-called wage-compensation-for-price-increases term, p_{cg}, labour productivity, a_g, the burden of taxation and social insurance contributions, (TL+PL)/L, and the change in the unemployment perunage, $\Delta U/a$ as determinants. Additionally, with the aid of dummy variables, the equation allows for special developments and wage controls in the 1970s, such as the Fl. 400 payment in 1970, the unbridled wage developments after the first oil crisis, despite the cyclical downswing at that time, and the harsh winter of 1979. This harsh winter has been accounted for because frost unemployment benefits are not counted as part of the wage and salary bill.

Apart from dummy variables and a constant term, the estimated wage equation for enterprises is:

$$\ln l_b^g = 0.925 \ln p_{cg} + 0.86 \ln a_g + 0.46 \ln ((TL + PL)/L) -$$

$$- 0.71 \left(\tfrac{1}{2} \sum_{j=0}^{1} \Delta \frac{U}{a}_{-j}\right)$$

Even though, government controls apart, the wage compensation for price increases was automatic and nearly 100 % during the observation period, the elasticity of the relevant term has been set lower than one, viz at 0.925. An important argument for this choice is that the price index actually used for wage compensation differs correspondingly from the price index for private consumption included in the model (another point is that, from 1977 onwards, price increases due to additional indirect taxation are not included in the index actually used). In the wage-compensation-for-price-increases term, p_{cg}, the lagged effect of price increases on wages has been accounted for in the following manner:

$$p_{cg} = p_{cg_{-1}} (1 + \alpha (p_{c_{-1}} - p_{c_{-3}})/p_{c_{-3}})$$

In this equation, p_c represents the price of private consumption, and α a vector with quarterly weights summing to one to allow for institutional aspects concerning the inclusion of the wage compensation for price increases in collective labour agreements. In the definition of labour productivity relevant for wages:

$$a_g = a_{g_{-1}} \left(1 + \tfrac{1}{4} \sum_{j=0}^{3} \left(\frac{y_{bm}}{a} - \frac{y_{bm_{-4}}}{a_{-4}}\right) / \left(\frac{y_{bm_{-4}}}{a_{-4}}\right)_{-j} \cdot \beta\right)$$

where y_{bm} represents the gross value added in enterprises and a employment, an analogous vector, β, serves to represent elements of collective bargaining practice.

The estimation results for the above wage equation also show that an increase in labour productivity is not reflected in full in wages. The burden of taxation and social insurance contributions is shifted for about one-half and the Phillips-curve effect found is fairly slight.

During the reference period, public servants' wages were determined mainly by their linkage to private sector wages. Apart from some specific and seasonal dummy variables, the percentage change in the wage and salary bill per public servant, $\dot{i}_{ov}$, has therefore been related only to the percentage change in the wage and salary bill per worker in enterprises:

$$\dot{i}_{ov} = 0.87\, \dot{i}_b^g$$

Owing to divergent developments with respect to wage drift, employers' contributions to social insurance and public servants' pay deductions in the late 1970s, the above elasticity is lower than one, viz 0.87.

3.3.4 *Output*

In the macro-economic models for the Netherlands, actual output is usually the sum of the various expenditure components determined in individual behavioural equations. MORKMON departs from this tradition. Following Fair (1976), a separate behavioural equation has been specified for the volume of gross output of enterprises, y. This equation is based on the theory of entrepreneurial behaviour. According to this theory, output is determined by expected sales and the desired level of stocks. Consequently, an output equation is specified with actual sales of enterprises, v_b, and the level of stocks at the beginning of the quarter, Σn_{-1}, as the explanatory variables, the (adaptive) expectations being incorporated by means of a Koyck lag. Apart from a constant term, seasonal dummy variables and the adjustment for the 1977 revision of the National Accounts, the estimation result of this equation is:

$$y = 0.16\, y_{-1} + 0.97\, v_b - 0.13\, \Sigma n_{-1}$$

The coefficient of y_{-1} shows that output adjusts very rapidly to expected sales.

As the model includes a behavioural equation for output, there is no need for a behavioural equation for stockbuilding, n. Stockbuilding follows from output and sales of enterprises:

$$n = y - v_b$$

This manner of modelling corresponds with the confrontation of income and expenditure underlying the model and with the treatment of stockbuilding as a residual item in the National Accounts, from which this confrontation has been derived. Moreover, as a behavioural relationship, the stockbuilding equation is among the most problematic relationships, both theoretically and empirically, in macro-economics.

3.3.5 Price determination

Apart from wage determination, price determination is described in MORKMON by six price equations [equations (70) to (75)], viz for the prices of:

. private consumption
. other gross fixed investment
. exports of goods
. autonomous expenditure
. investment in dwellings
. stockbuilding

These price equations are based on the reasoning that prices reflect production costs and import prices of final products. Additionally, a role is played by the rate of capacity utilization, and the prices of competitive products. A low rate of capacity utilization tends to depress prices. The principal equations concern the prices of consumer goods, investment and exports. The price equations for autonomous government expenditure, investment in dwellings and stockbuilding, are to some extent identities. The estimated equations are expressed in percentage changes, so that constant elasticities have been assumed.

In the equation for the price of private consumption, p_c, the lag with regard to the wage variable, ι_b^g, has been set at half a quarter to ensure plausible estimation results, and the elasticity with regard to the import price, p_{mc}, has been set at 0.2. Furthermore, the equation includes the increase in labour productivity, $(\dot{y}_{bm}-\dot{a})$, as a determinant and a number of dummy variables, which are not discussed here. It was found that the rate of capacity utilization and the price of capital could not be suitably included in this equation; hence, they have been left out. The estimated equation is as follows:

$$\dot{p}_c = 0.47\,(½ \sum_{j=0}^{1} \dot{i}^g_{b_{-j}}) - 0.12\,(\dot{y}_{bm} - \dot{a}) + 0.20\,\dot{p}_{mc}$$

This estimation result shows a coefficient for the increase in labour productivity which is considerably lower than the coefficient for wages. The sum of the wage and price elasticities is 0.67, so that the equation is not homogeneous.

In the above equation the coefficient of the import price has been set at 0.2, because free estimation did not produce plausible results. The choice is based on the consideration that a change in the price of imports is reflected to an average extent of about 20 % in a change in the price of private consumption. However, this means that the wage coefficient and the price coefficient do not sum to one. For that reason, an alternative equation has been estimated for the price of private consumption which does meet this requirement of homogeneity; this has been achieved by imposing this requirement when estimating the equation. Apart from a constant term and dummy variables, this equation, which has been included as an alternative in Appendix I, is as follows:

$$\dot{p}_c = 0.78\,(½ \sum_{j=0}^{1} \dot{i}^g_{b_{-j}}) - 0.14\,(\dot{y}_{bm} - \dot{a}) + 0.22\,\dot{p}_{mc}$$

In the equation for the price of other gross fixed investment of enterprises, $p_{i_{-sa}}$, the length of the lags has also been determined *a priori* in order to obtain plausible results. Apart from dummy variables, the estimated equation is:

$$\dot{p}_{i_{-sa}} = 0.39\,(½ \sum_{j=0}^{1} \dot{i}^g_{b_{-j}}) - 0.14\,(\dot{y}_{bm} - \dot{a}) + 0.42\,(¼ \sum_{j=0}^{3} \dot{p}_{mi_{-j}}) +$$

$$+ 0.05\,\dot{p}_k + 0.22\,(¼ \sum_{j=0}^{3} \dot{q}_{k_{-j}})$$

Unlike the previous one, this equation includes the price of capital, p_k, and the utilization rate of capital, q_k, as explanatory variables, while foreign costs are represented by the price of imports of capital goods, p_{mi}. The estimation result shows that in this equation, too, the effect of labour productivity is relatively small. The sum of the wage and price elasticities is 0.86, so that this equation is not homogeneous either. The equation for the price of exports of goods (excluding ships, aircraft, oil and gas), $p_{b_{-saog}}$, is:

$$\dot{p}_{b_{-saog}} = 0.22\, \dot{i}^{g}_{b_{-1}} - 0.31\, (\dot{y}_{bm} - \dot{a}) + 0.17\, (\tfrac{1}{2} \sum_{j=0}^{1} \dot{p}_{mgh_{-j}}) + 0.13\, \dot{p}_{k_{-1}} +$$

$$+ 0.49\, \dot{p}_{bf} + 0.51\, (\tfrac{1}{4} \sum_{j=0}^{3} \dot{q}_{k_{-j}})$$

Again, the plausibility of the results has in part determined the lag structure. Besides the import price of raw materials and intermediate goods, p_{mgh}, which is mainly important as a cost factor, the export price of competitor countries, p_{bf}, has been included as an explanatory variable, as pricing by Dutch exporters partly depends on prices prevailing on the world market. Finally, the estimation result in this equation suggests (practically) homogeneous pricing.

The other three price equations are derived ones. They establish a link with the other endogenous prices discussed above and import prices, first-degree homogeneity having been imposed.

The price of autonomous expenditure, p_x, is determined by the price of private consumption, p_c, the import price, $p_{m_{-saog}}$, and the price of investment, $p_{i_{-sa}}$:

$$\dot{p}_x = 0.51\, \dot{p}_c + 0.19\, \dot{p}_{m_{-saog}} + 0.30\, \dot{p}_{i_{-sa}}$$

For the price of investment in dwellings, $p_{i_{wo}}$, the following equation holds:

$$\dot{p}_{i_{wo}} = 0.40\, \dot{p}_i + 0.60\, \dot{p}_c$$

where p_i represents the price of gross fixed investment of enterprises and p_c the price of private consumption.

The price of stockbuilding, p_n, is determined by the price of private consumption, p_c, and the import price, p_m:

$$\dot{p}_n = 0.29\, \dot{p}_c + 0.71\, \dot{p}_m$$

Finally, the results for the three most important price equations are summarized in Table 3.2 in the form of elasticities. The wage and price elasticities sum to 0.67, 0.86 and 1.01, respectively. Thus only the export price equation is practically homogeneous.

Table 3.2
Elasticities of three price equations

Equation for	Elasticity with regard to				
	wage costs	labour productivity	import price/price of competitive goods	capital costs	utilization rate of capital
Price of private consumption	0.47	-0.12	0.20		
Price of investment	0.39	-0.14	0.42	0.05	0.22
Price of exports	0.22	-0.31	0.66	0.13	0.51

3.3.6 *Income distribution and the public sector*

Factor and disposable incomes are described by a number of technical equations and identities, which are usual in macro-economic models.

Regarding factor income, the total wage and salary bill is the total of the wage and salary bill in enterprises and that of the government [equation (191)]. The wage and salary bill in each of these two sectors is obtained by multiplying employment by the wage and salary bill per wage earner determined in the relevant wage equations [equations (103) and (104)]. In the model, other income is calculated as a residual item, viz as the difference between value added and the wage and salary bill in enterprises [equation (105)]. The self-employed, constituting a separate category receiving other income, have been imputed a wage and salary bill per worker which is equal to that of the employees [equation (107)].

With regard to disposable income, tax revenues are determined by four technical relationships. The first three equations [equations (113) to (115)] describe direct taxes in respect of wage income, transfer income and other income, respectively. Indirect taxes [equation (116)] have been netted out with price-reducing subsidies and price-increasing levies, related to total expenditure.

For social security, a sub-model has been designed, endogenizing the transfer income paid by the government on the one hand, and benefits and payments disbursed by social insurance funds, pension funds and life assurance companies on the other. The benefits and payments have been split up into a 'price' component and a 'volume' component. The price component is represented by the wage and salary bill per worker in enterprises, l_b^g, so that payments and benefits are thus linked to wages. The volume has been assumed to be endogenous in part only, viz in the case of unemployment benefits where the number of recipients of benefits depends upon unemployment. Here, a distinction has been made between recipients of unemployment benefits paid by the social insurance funds, and recipients of other unemployment benefits paid by the government.

The number of (fully) unemployed persons receiving benefits under the Unemployment Act, WW, has been made dependent not only on the level of unemployment, U, itself, but also on the increase in unemployment, $\Delta_4 U$ [equation (76)]. With increasing unemployment, the share of the long- term unemployed receiving benefits paid by the government increases. However, initially they are entitled for a period of six months to benefits under the Unemployment Act. Consequently, an increase in unemployment leads to a temporary increase in benefits under the Unemployment Act. Apart from a constant term and seasonal dummy variables, the estimation result for this equation is:

$$WW = 0.15\ U + 0.28\ \Delta_4 U$$

The benefits under the Unemployment Act are described in equation (118), while the benefits paid to the other unemployed by the government under the Unemployment Provisions Act and the Government Scheme for Unemployed Employees, (U-WW), are determined in equation (121).

The other benefits and payments disbursed by the social insurance funds, pension funds and life assurance companies and the other government income transfers (mainly social assistance payments and subsidies) are made dependent on the wage and salary bill per worker only [equations (119) and (122)]. Aggregation of all these benefits and payments yields total transfer income [equation (124)]. The total payments made by the social insurance funds, pension funds and life assurance companies [equation (120)] and the costs of these institutions, less the central government's transfers to social insurance, are financed from premiums [equation (125)]. Equations (126) to (128) allocate these premiums among the wage and salary bill, recipients of benefits and the self-employed.

Confrontation of factor income with premiums and taxes paid and benefits received yields disposable income for the various categories [equations (129) to (135)].

3.4. Comparison of elasticities for external trade

When the model equations were estimated, in a number of cases comparisons were made with corresponding estimates found in other studies relating to the Netherlands. This procedure was notably followed with regard to the equations for exports and imports of goods.

Table 3.3 presents a survey of some export elasticities with respect to world trade and relative prices. For these elasticities, the export equation in MORKMON implies values of 0.98 and –1.2, respectively. Table 3.3 shows that notably the price substitu-

Table 3.3
Elasticities in the export equation of some models for the Netherlands

Model	Estimation period	Elasticity	
		world trade	export price
1 Van den Beld (1968)	1953-1963	1.01	–
2 Brandsma/Van der Windt (1980)	annual figures	0.98	-2.28
3 CPB 69C [CPB (1971)]	1921-1969	0.85	-2.39
4 CPB quarterly [Driehuis (1972)]	1951:I-1965:IV	0.93	-2.05
5 CPB quarterly-re-estimated [Fase *et al.* (1976)]	1961:I-1973:IV	1.05	-1.02
6 Groot/Janssen (1979)	1962-1977	0.75	-2.63
7 Knoester (1977)	1953-1974	0.91	-1.81
8 Knoester (1980)	1953-1975	0.77	-1.28
9 VINTAF-II [CPB (1977)]	1960-1973	1.07	-1.69
10 FREIA [Hasselman, Okker en Den Haan (1983)]	1954-1978	1.0	-2.0

tion elasticity of -1.2 is low in absolute terms, compared with the corresponding estimates in other models.

Table 3.4 presents a survey of sales and price elasticities for imports resulting from a number of studies of Dutch imports. Comparison shows that the corresponding values in the import equation in MORKMON regarding sales and prices of 0.99 and -0.74, respectively, correspond fairly with a number of values shown in the Table.

Table 3.4
Elasticities in the import equation of some models for the Netherlands

Model	Estimation period	Elasticity	
		sales	import price
1 CPB 69C [CPB (1981)]	1921-1969	1.06	-0.35
2 CPB quarterly [Driehuis (1972)]	1951:I-1965:IV	1.00	-0.70
3 CPB quarterly-re-estimated [Fase *et al.* (1976)]	1961:I-1973:IV	1.30	-0.51
4 Knoester (1980)	1953-1975	0.83	-0.19
5 VINTAF-II [CPB (1977)]	1960-1973	1.11	-0.51

4 The links between the monetary and the real economic sector

The models described in the preceding Chapters are partial in the sense that, in their description, their interaction has been ignored.

The connection between the monetary and the real economic sector is most evident in the financing summary discussed in Chapter 2 (Table 2.1), which describes the financial balances by sector. The Table can be summarized by the accounting identity:

$$\Delta V_{ps} + \Delta V_{b} + \Delta V_{cb} - FT_{o} - LR = 0$$

which can, apart from statistical discrepancies and items in transit, be derived directly from equation (51). The counterpart of this identity is the macro-economic budget constraint, which constitutes the principal bridge between the real economic sector, where the formation of real wealth takes place, and the monetary sector, where the resultant financial changes are described. In the same way as equation (51) summarizes the monetary sector, the macro-economic budget constraint summarizes the real economic sector. The relevant relationship can be written as:

$$(S_{p} - I) - FT_{o}^{tr} - E = 0$$

where $(S_p - I)$ represents the savings surpluses, FT_o^{tr} the government's financial deficit and E the balance on current account, all on a transactions basis. The link of FT_o^{tr} and E with the corresponding variables in the monetary sector is established by means of identities (158) and (27).

In addition to the above relationships, there are a large number of technically indispensable but economically less important relationships which give shape to the connection. Most of them are identities or accounting relationships which are not very informative from an economic point of view but are needed for the operation of the integrated model.

Linking the two sub-models means that the monetary transmission from the financial to the real economic sector and vice versa is made visible. For example, in the traditional macro-economic IS-LM model, the interest rate is the sole transmission channel. In more comprehensively specified macro-economic models, however, not only the interest rate but also monetary quantitative variables and relative prices, including exchange rates, have a direct effect on the real economic sector. In such models the effects of the real economic on the monetary sector are likewise manifold, not least because income, inflation, international trade and government deficits are of major significance for the explanation of changes in financial wealth.

The monetary transmission channels distinguished in MORKMON, after weighing up theoretical and empirical considerations, concern both interest rate and quantitative variables. Additionally, relative prices play a role. The interest rate directly affects the domestic expenditure categories, consumption and investment in dwellings and other fixed investment, as well as the price of capital. Furthermore, other fixed investment is influenced by liquidity conditions, measured in terms of the liquidity ratio, and the degree of external financing in enterprises. These liquidity conditions, as far as they are represented by the liquidity ratio, could not be shown to have an effect on consumption. The same holds, though in a broader scope, for the effect of credit restrictions on expenditure.

In the model the monetary transmission through relative prices is reflected in the effect of changes in exchange rates. The exchange rate of the guilder, which is, incidentally, subject within the European Monetary System to a limited margin of fluctuation against the Deutsche mark, influences import prices. Modelling has been effected by eight technical relationships [equations (143) to (150)], which convert exogenous foreign-currency import prices into guilder prices as follows:

$$p_m = \underline{p}_m \cdot e_{\$}^{\alpha} \cdot e_{DM}^{\beta}$$

These technical relationships – the presentation of their general form may suffice here – ensure that changes in exchange rates feed through into import prices in a consistent manner. The effects of the dollar's and the Deutsche mark's exchange rate on guilder import prices, α and β, respectively, have been determined for each category of imports on the basis of trade flows as an approximation of the extent of invoicing in dollars and Deutsche marks.

Another, interesting channel of monetary transmission concerns the interest payments on government debt, Re. Actually, the monetary transmission referred to here is but one side of the interaction between the real economic and the monetary sector. The other is that, even though government debt itself, and the interest payments as an integral part of it, are determined in the real economic sector, the manner of financing is described in the monetary block. The monetary transmission is described by equations (156) and (157). The first is:

$$Re = \bar{r}\ (VAS + VLS)$$

and is an identity, defining the government's interest payments as the product of an average interest rate, $\bar{r}$, and total long and short-term government debt, (VAS + VLS). The second equation is:

$$\bar{r} = 0.782 \left(\sum_{j=4}^{64} \pi_{-j} \cdot r_{l_{-j}} \right) + 0.100 \left({}^{1}\!/\!_{20} \sum_{j=0}^{19} r_{sc_{-j}} \right) + 0.097\, r_k$$

It defines the average interest rate as a weighted average of the three interest rates which are most relevant to the financing of government debt. The lag structure reflects the importance of historical interest rates at which the debt was financed in the course of time. Here, the variable π is related to the quarterly survival fraction of debt, and hence $1-\pi$ to the fraction of debt repayments (the weights π_{-j} sum to one). The actual equation in Appendix I includes not only a constant term but also seasonal dummy variables, because interest payments and, consequently, the average interest rate exhibit a seasonal pattern.

Much has been said and written about the monetary transmission channels [cf. e.g. Den Butter (1981) for an empirical survey]. Within the framework of a macroeconomic model such as the one described here, these channels of transmission are in the first instance determined by the empirical findings in the individual equations. Their significance as monetary transmission channels within the integrated model as a whole will only become apparent by simulation analysis conducted with the entire model as well as with the individual blocks.

5 The integrated model and its descriptive power

5.1 The ex post operation of the model

Any model must at the very least be able to reproduce the past. To test the model's performance in this respect, this section and the next review the results of dynamic simulation or *ex post* forecasting for the main variables. Using the simultaneous model, dynamic simulation generates a time profile for the endogenous variables of the model on the basis of historical initial values for the lagged endogenous variables; subsequently, these variables are assigned the values generated by the model. For the exogenous variables, historical values are used. It is evident that dynamic simulation puts a model to a most exacting test. Moreover, such simulation affords some insight into the dynamics of the model. The present section is concerned with the overall fit of the complete model as well as of the two sub-models. The fit is summarized in two alternative statistics. The next section presents a graphic comparison between simulated and historical time paths for the main variables.

There are various ways of summarizing the overall fit of a model in a statistic. These ways concern both the criterion used and the unit in which the *ex post* prediction in question (and the criterion) is expressed. Below, the unit of each statistic corresponds to the unit of the respective endogeneous variable in the model. This means that in cases where the model generates an absolute or percentage change the statistic presented is expressed correspondingly. This serves to prevent the statistics used from giving a flattered picture of the model's ability.

The statistics used here are Theil's inequality coefficient and the mean prediction error, defined as:

$$\frac{\sqrt{\Sigma\,(v_t - r_t)^2}}{\sqrt{\Sigma\, v_t^2} + \sqrt{\Sigma\, r_t^2}}$$

and

$$\frac{1}{n}\,\Sigma\,(v_t - r_t)^2$$

respectively, where v_t represents the value predicted by the model and r_t the actual value of the variable during period t or at moment t, with $t=1,\ldots,n$. The two statistics,

Table 5.1
Inequality coefficients and mean prediction errors in MORKMON (1971:II-1982:IV)

Variable	Theil's inequality coefficient	Mean prediction error
M2/FA	0.238	0.004
S/FA	0.246	0.003
LK_{ps}/FA	0.088	0.002
BNIB/FA	0.165	0.002
CH/M2	0.308	0.005
D/M2	0.247	0.015
TV/M2	0.405	0.026
KOS_{ps}/M2	0.417	0.004
BL	0.005	0.109
LOG_{ps}	0.087	0.861
$LK_{b,ps}$	0.350	0.002
$BTB \mid S_{fs}$	0.139	1.396
S_b	0.032	0.040
BBIN	0.200	0.655
NBA_b	0.447	3.639
ΔHKO_{bu}	0.429	0.022
ΔHKV_{bu}	0.324	0.018
r_k	0.076	1.216
r_l	0.022	0.405
r_d	0.075	0.192
r_s	0.028	0.254
r_{sc}	0.108	1.463
r_{bl}	0.028	0.580
$\bar{r}$	0.034	0.517
$\dot{e}_{\$}$	0.129	1.215
c	0.035	2.743
i_{-sa}	0.045	0.641
i_{wo}	0.040	0.309
b_{-saog}	0.003	0.057
m_{-saog}	0.003	0.064
y	0.027	4.882
a	0.010	0.081
a_a	0.004	0.040
ι^{g}_{b}	0.014	0.063
$\dot{\iota}_{ov}$	0.229	1.444
$\dot{p}_c$	0.243	0.993
$\dot{p}_{i_{-sa}}$	0.272	1.055
$\dot{p}_{b_{-saog}}$	0.273	1.446
$\dot{p}_x$	0.201	0.908
$\dot{p}_{i_{wo}}$	0.220	1.064
$\dot{p}_n$	0.146	9.204
WW	0.174	0.026

calculated for the period 1971:II-1982:IV for all variables determined by behavioural relationships, are given in Table 5.1. With regard to this Table, it might be noted that, unlike Theil's inequality coefficient, the mean prediction error is sensitive to the unit in which the variable is expressed. Consequently, the mean prediction error is less suitable for purposes of comparison. Therefore the inequality coefficient is preferred as the criterion for assessment. Secondly, it must be borne in mind that, for a number of variables, the period 1971:II-1982:IV employed in the Table is longer than the actual sample period. Hence, in such cases, the Table gives an impression not only of the *ex post* predictive performance but also of the *ex ante* predictive performance, albeit with historical values for the exogenous variables. This logically weakens the predictive performance.

Classification by magnitude of the inequality coefficients presented in Table 5.1 results in a striking U-shaped pattern (Table 5.2).

Table 5.2
Summary of inequality coefficients of MORKMON

Class	Number
0.0 < 0.05	15
0.05 < 0.10	5
0.10 < 0.20	5
0.20 < 0.50	17
	42

Closer inspection shows that the low values often relate to real economic variables, whereas the high values practically always relate to financial wealth variables. The interest rate, price and exchange rate variables are consistently somewhere in between.

This picture does not alter drastically if the descriptive power of the two blocks, viz REKMON (real economic block) and MOKMON (monetary block), is considered separately (Table 5.3). As expected, this produces a marginal decrease in the statistics for most of the variables.
This means that in these cases the integration of the monetary and the real economic sub-model leads to a lower predictive performance than that of the component parts. However, for a limited number of variables, integration proves to enhance descriptive power. It is noteworthy that this is apparent for nearly all variables from the real economic block. For the variables from the monetary block, the situation is more varied, because for four variables (D, KOS_{ps}, $LK_{fs,gb}$ and BBIN) integration leads to lower descriptive power. It would appear justified to conclude that integration does not materially affect the *ex post* forecasting power of the two sub-models.

Table 5.3
Inequality coefficients and mean prediction errors in REKMON and MOKMON (1971:II-1982:IV)

Variable	REKMON		MOKMON	
	Theil's inequality coefficient	Mean prediction error	Theil's inequality coefficient	Mean prediction error
M2/FA			0.238	0.004
S/FA			0.245	0.003
LK_{ps}/FA			0.094	0.003
BNIB/FA			0.172	0.002
CH/M2			0.334	0.006
D/M2			0.225	0.014
TV/M2			0.419	0.027
KOS_{ps}/M2			0.411	0.004
BL			0.002	0.042
LOG_{ps}			0.088	0.875
$LK_{b,ps}$			0.343	0.002
$BTB \mid S_{fs}$			0.138	1.359
S_b			0.030	0.038
BBIN			0.183	0.556
NBA_b			0.420	4.032
ΔHKO_{bu}			0.429	0.022
ΔHKV_{bu}			0.302	0.017
r_k			0.077	1.218
r_l			0.023	0.406
r_d			0.075	0.189
r_s			0.024	0.222
r_{sc}			0.110	1.461
r_{bl}			0.028	0.574
$\bar{r}$			0.034	0.514
$\dot{e}_{\$}$			0.130	1.228
c	0.035	2.789		
i_{-sa}	0.047	0.664		
i_{wo}	0.036	0.280		
b_{-saog}	0.003	0.055		
m_{-saog}	0.003	0.057		
y	0.027	4.873		
a	0.010	0.077		
a_a	0.004	0.040		
ι_b^g	0.015	0.065		
$\dot{\iota}_{ov}$	0.234	1.472		
$\dot{p}_c$	0.245	1.008		
$\dot{p}_{i_{-sa}}$	0.284	1.105		
$\dot{p}_{b_{-saog}}$	0.277	1.464		
$\dot{p}_x$	0.200	0.907		
$\dot{p}_{i_{wo}}$	0.219	1.059		
$\dot{p}_n$	0.149	9.361		
WW	0.181	0.027		

5.2 The operation of the model viewed graphically

To complement the general assessment of the model's descriptive power as presented in the preceding section, a graphic evaluation of the behavioural equations in MORKMON is presented here. For each variable, the time path generated by dynamic simulation with the complete model is compared with the historical time path. As far as possible, the sequence of these comparisons is the same as those of the presentation of the behavioural equations in the model and in Tables 5.1 and 5.3. In the Charts, the unbroken blue lines represent the historical time paths; the dotted red lines represent the time paths generated by simulation. Twelve series include a break, of which eight in 1977:I on account of the revision of the National Accounts and the remaining four in 1977:IV owing to the redefinition of the concept of savings deposits.

Charts 5.1 to 5.4 depict the quality of the equations in the model for the allocation of the private sector's financial assets among its four components: the domestic money stock, M2, savings deposits, S, capital market investments, LK_{ps}, and private sector holdings of foreign liabilities, BNIB. The left-hand Charts (5.1A to 5.4A) are in conformity with the relevant equations, being expressed in changes in shares. The right-hand Charts (5.1B to 5.4B) depict the resultant levels of the shares. The simulated time path proves to coincide fairly well with the historical time path for the sample period 1970:III-1982:IV used for these equations. There are no striking differences.

The allocation of the money stock among its components currency, CH, demand deposits, D, time and foreign-currency deposits, TV, and short-term government debt held by the private sector, KOS_{ps}, is described in Charts 5.5A to 5.8A. These Charts again show the changes in the shares, while the resultant levels of the shares are presented in Charts 5.5B to 5.8B. Inspection of the Charts reveals a number of striking differences between the historical and the simulated time path, e.g. for currency in 1977:IV and 1979:II, and for demand deposits in early 1977, when the shifting of funds between time deposits and savings accounts was topical. This is also the explanation of the major discrepancy between the simulated and the historical time path of time deposits in 1977; for this component of the money stock, major differences are also apparent in 1975:I, the second half of 1973, 1975 and recent years. In the Charts showing the levels of the shares, these differences are less obvious.

The simulated and the historical time path of short and long-term lending to the private sector is shown in Charts 5.9 and 5.10. Unlike in the underlying equations of the Charts discussed so far, the sample period used here does not extend beyond 1979:IV, so that the Charts also partly present *ex ante* forecasts, albeit that the values of the exogenous variables are historical. Short-term bank lending, for which the Chart presents levels, is marked by too high predictions in the recent periods. This could suggest a decrease in the elasticity with regard to sales, which is very high in the estimated equation for the demand for short-term bank loans. For long-term lending the picture is slightly better – also outside the estimation period – owing largely to the fact that this equation is specified in changes. Chart 5.11 depicts the changes in the ratio of the banks' capital market investments to the long-term funds raised by the private sector. The model describes the time profile fairly well, although outside the sample period the simulated time path is consistently higher than the actual one. This phenomenon is also apparent for the changes in the balance sheet total of the institutional investors, $BTB \mid S_{fs}$, shown in Chart 5.12. The simulated time path is much smoother than the historical one, which shows a number of wide fluctuations, for instance at the end of 1974. This is, incidentally, largely due to the strongly aggregated nature of this variable, which is, moreover, subject to breaks in series. Large discrepancies between the simulated and the historical time path also occur for the share of savings deposits with money-creating institutions in total savings deposits, S_b/S. Chart 5.13 shows, incidentally, that the discrepancies outside the sample period (in this case 1970:II-1979:IV) are a continuation of the model's underprediction from 1978 onwards.

Apart from the private sector's holdings of foreign liabilities shown in Chart 5.4, the external capital transactions are presented in Charts 5.14 to 5.17. Chart 5.14 shows that for foreign holdings of domestic liabilities, BBIN, the simulated results are fairly in line with the historical pattern. This also holds for the quarters of 1982, which are outside the sample period for this equation. The picture presented by Chart 5.15, which shows the levels of the banking system's net foreign assets, NBA_b, is less satisfactory. At the end of the sample period 1970:II -1979:IV, underprediction of the historical pattern is discernible, while for the subsequent periods the simulated time path is consistently higher than the actual one. This could possibly be due to the persistent current-account surpluses recorded since 1980, which differ substantially from those in the sample period. Inspection of the individual equation proves that it performs well until 1983. This means that the prediction errors are wholly the result of the simultaneity. External trade credit received and granted are shown in Charts 5.16 and 5.17. In this case, too, the discrepancies between the simulated and the actual pattern increase after the end of the sample period (here 1970:III-1979:IV). However, they do not seem to be disquieting, the more so as these equations describe changes.

The various endogenous interest rates described by the model are depicted in Charts 5.18 to 5.24. Charts 5.18 and 5.19 – the short-term and the long-term interest rate – both show a satisfactory picture. However, for the long-term interest rate, the moderate descriptive power at the start of the sample period (1971:II-1982:IV) is noteworthy. Chart 5.20, which represents the interest rate on current-account deposits, shows a striking difference between the historical and the simulated time profile after 1979:IV, that is, outside the sample period used for this equation. This is no doubt due to the relative rigidity of this interest rate after 1979. As evidenced by Chart 5.21, the interest rate on savings deposits, which is likewise relatively rigid, sometimes shows striking differences between the simulated and actual time path. Nevertheless, the model's results correspond closely to actual developments, even outside the sample period 1970:II-1979:IV. The same is true of the interest rate on three-month Treasury paper depicted in Chart 5.22 and of the interest rate on short-term bank loans shown in Chart 5.23. Finally, Chart 5.24 shows the average interest rate on government debt, which in MORKMON represents a link with the real economic sector. The fit is good, which is not surprising since the same holds for the long-term interest rate; this is, incidentally, largely due to the calculation method used in the equation concerned. Nor is it a surprise to note the good performance of the model for the percentage changes in the dollar's exchange rate, illustrated in Chart 5.25, for which the sample period was 1970:III-1982:IV. This predictive performance is attributable to the fact that the principal explanatory variable, the exchange rate of the dollar against the Deutsche mark, is exogenous.

The first 33 Charts relate to the monetary endogenous variables in the integrated model which have been determined by behavioural equations. The remaining 17 Charts describe the time paths of the model's principal real economic endogenous variables for the period 1971:II-1982:IV. Unlike in MORKMON's monetary sub-model MOKMON, the sample period for each estimated equation in the real economic sub-model REKMON is 1970:I-1979:IV. Consequently, the quarters after 1979:IV afford an insight into the model's *ex ante* forecasting power, albeit with historical values for the exogenous variables.

Charts 5.26 to 5.29 describe the simulated and the historical time path of the expenditure categories. Generally, the *ex post* forecasts are fairly good. However, the *ex ante* forecasts are less satisfactory, which is not alarming if it is realized that, in the case of dynamic simulation, any discrepancy tends to continue for a long time. This is a major difference compared with actual forecasting practice, where the forecasts are invariably based on the most recent data available.

Charts 5.30 to 5.33 depict production and the factors of production. The equation for employment, in particular, shows major discrepancies between simulated and actual values. This is largely due to the fact that in the labour demand equation where the endogenously determined rate of capacity utilization plays an important role, the simulated data differ considerably from the figures used in the single estimation equation. Wages and prices are described in Charts 5.34 to 5.41. A few exceptions apart, the simulated time path corresponds fairly closely to the historical profile. Only in a few quarters do some rather large discrepancies occur for the price of other fixed investment and the price of investment in dwellings. A noteworthy feature is the close correspondence between the simulated and the actual time path of the price level of stockbuilding, a variable with a residual character. The residual character of this variable incidentally explains the rather erratic actual time profile. Chart 5.42 shows the time path of the number of unemployed persons receiving benefits under the Unemployment Act, and reveals fairly large discrepancies between simulated and historical values, notably in 1980, that is, outside the sample period.

All in all, this graphic inspection teaches that MORKMON is fairly well capable of reproducing reality, a conclusion which warrants confidence in the model. It must be pointed out, however, that the model's good performance in describing the past does not necessarily mean that it can do the same for the future. Nevertheless, it must be acknowledged that the performance for the past inspires confidence.

Chart 5.1A
Domestic money stock
(changes as % of financial assets)

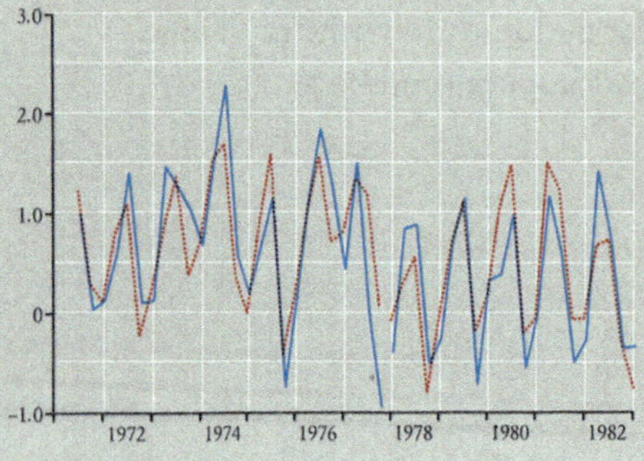

Chart 5.1B
Domestic money stock
(% of financial assets)

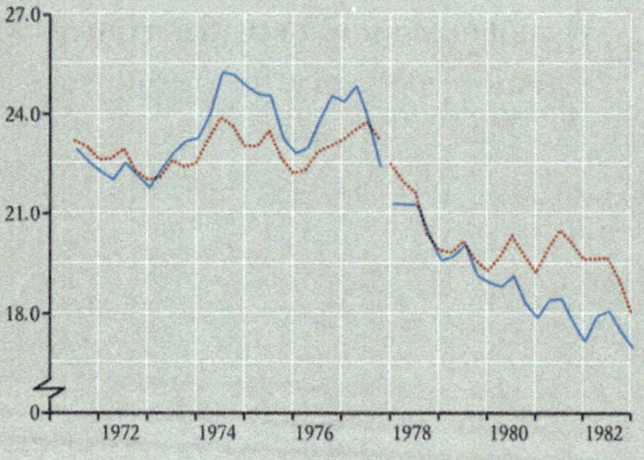

Chart 5.2A
Savings deposits
(changes as % of financial assets)

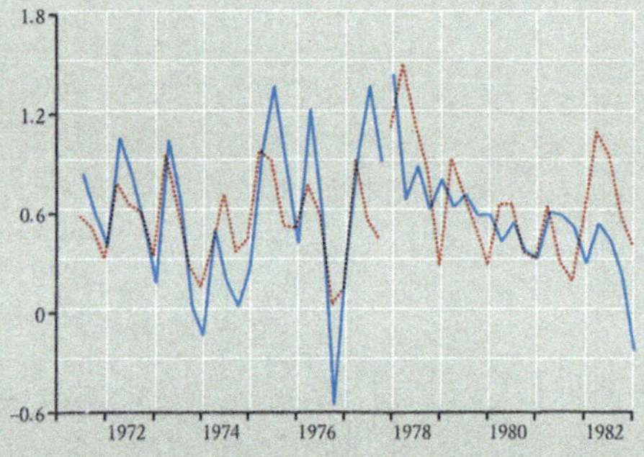

Chart 5.2B
Savings deposits
(% of financial assets)

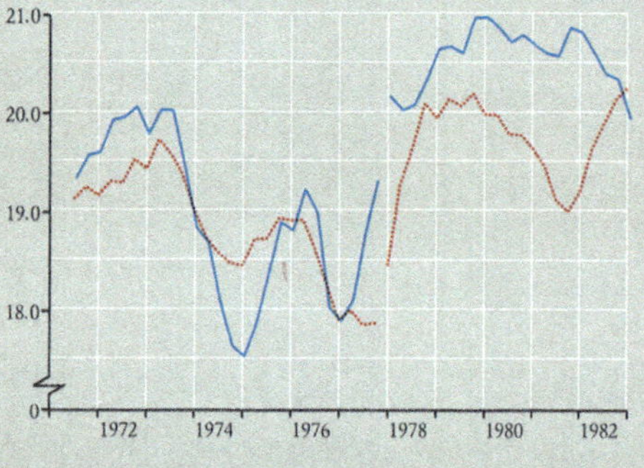

Chart 5.3A
Capital market investment of the private sector
(changes as % of financial assets)

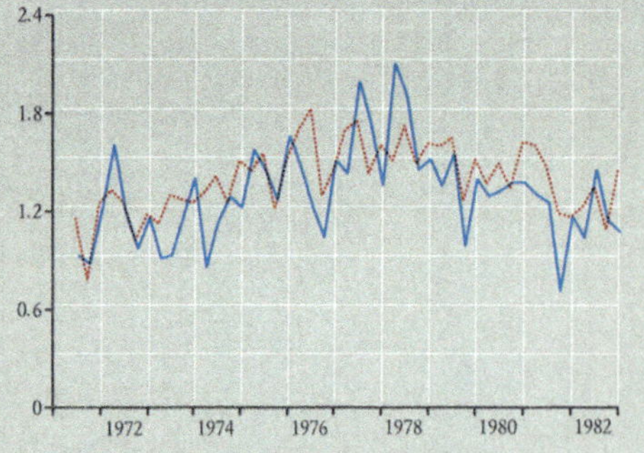

Chart 5.3B
Capital market investment of the private sector
(% of financial assets)

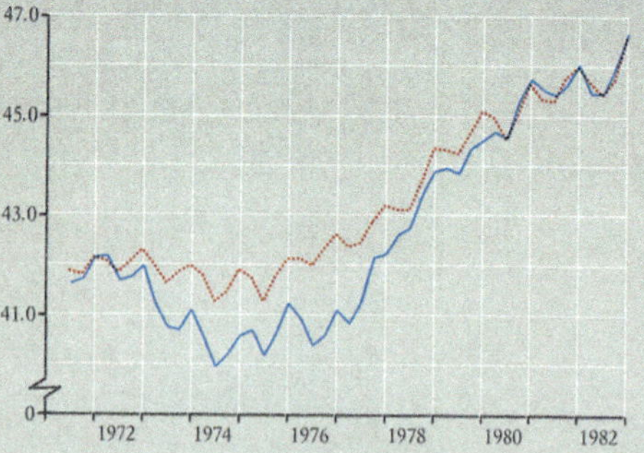

——— historical time path
········ simulated time path

Chart 5.4A
Private sector holdings of foreign liabilities
(changes as % of financial assets)

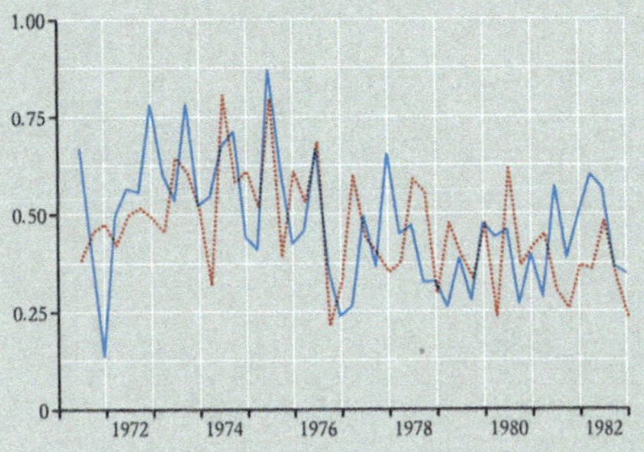

Chart 5.4B
Private sector holdings of foreign liabilities
(% of financial assets)

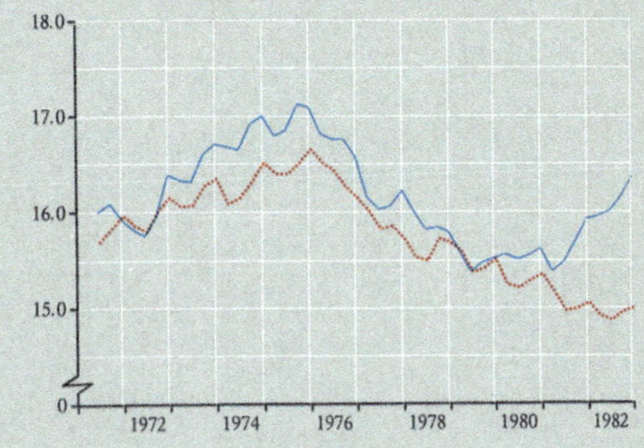

Chart 5.5A
Currency
(changes as % of domestic money stock)

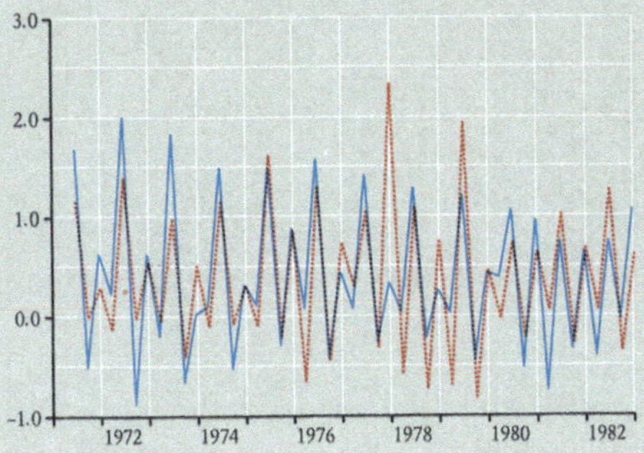

Chart 5.5B
Currency
(% of domestic money stock)

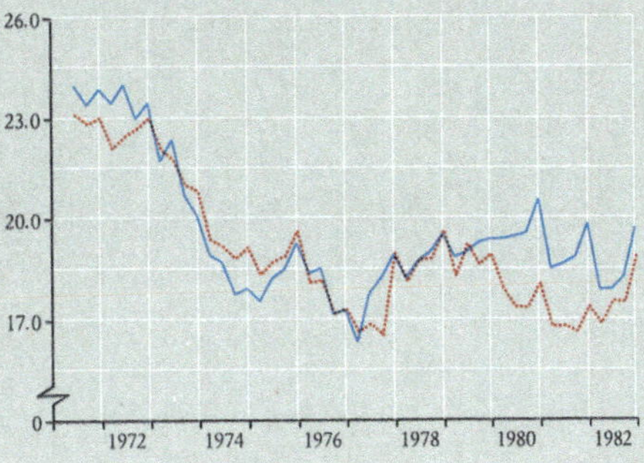

Chart 5.6A
Demand deposits
(changes as % of domestic money stock)

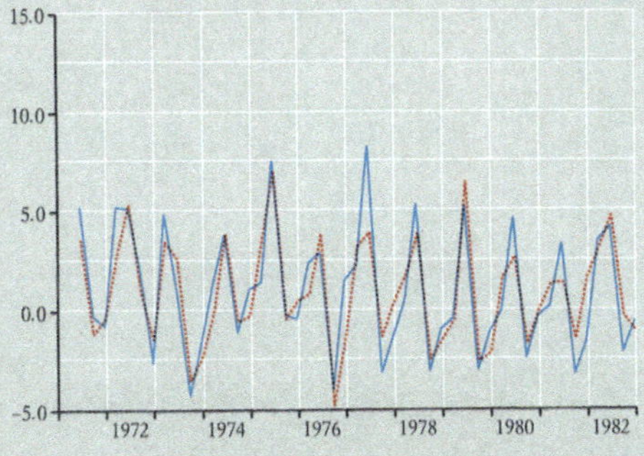

Chart 5.6B
Demand deposits
(% of domestic money stock)

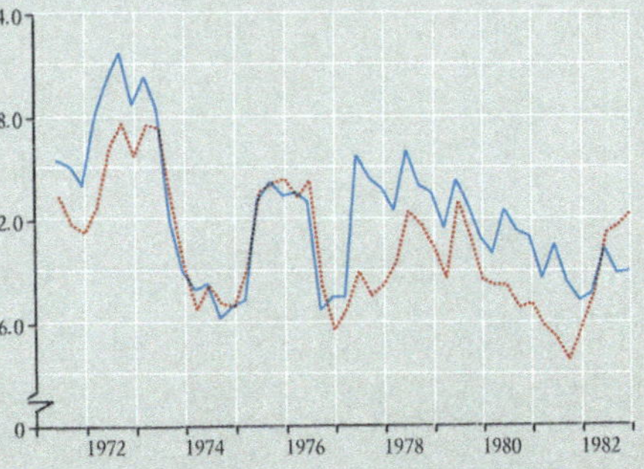

historical time path
simulated time path

Chart 5.7A
Time deposits and foreign-currency deposits
(changes as % of domestic money stock)

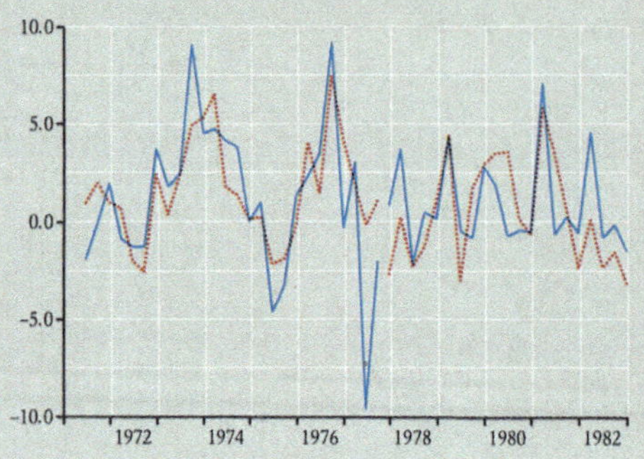

Chart 5.7B
Time deposits and foreign-currency deposits
(% of domestic money stock)

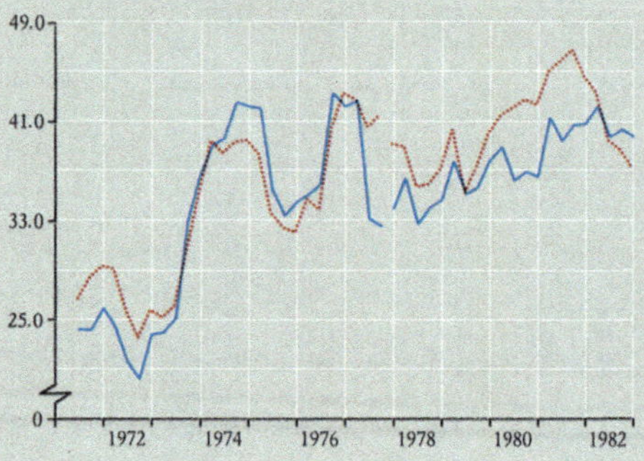

Chart 5.8A
Short-term government debt held by the private sector
(changes as % of domestic money stock)

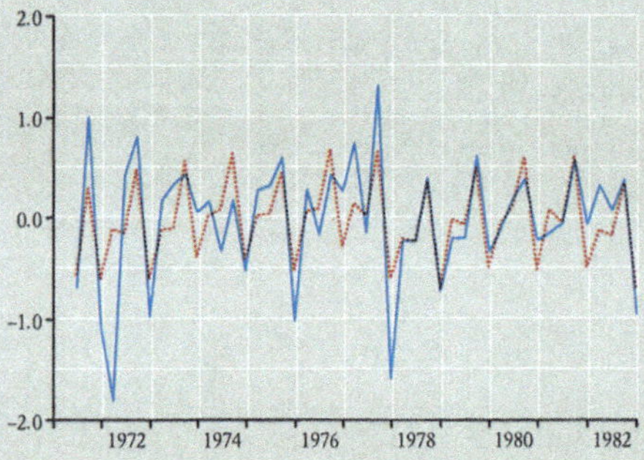

Chart 5.8B
Short-term government debt held by the private sector
(% of domestic money stock)

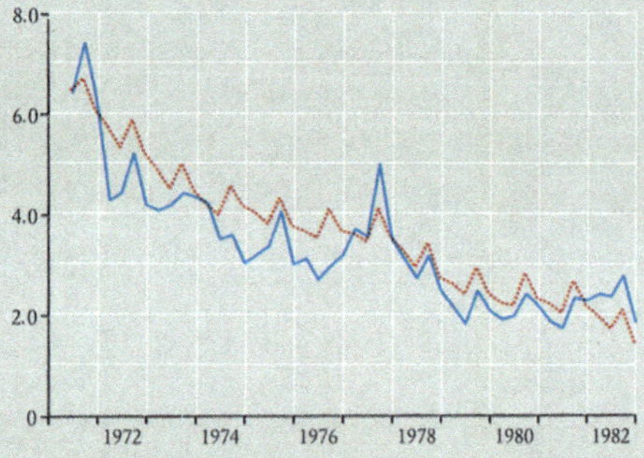

Chart 5.9
Short-term bank lending to the private sector
(nat. log. of amounts in millions of guilders)

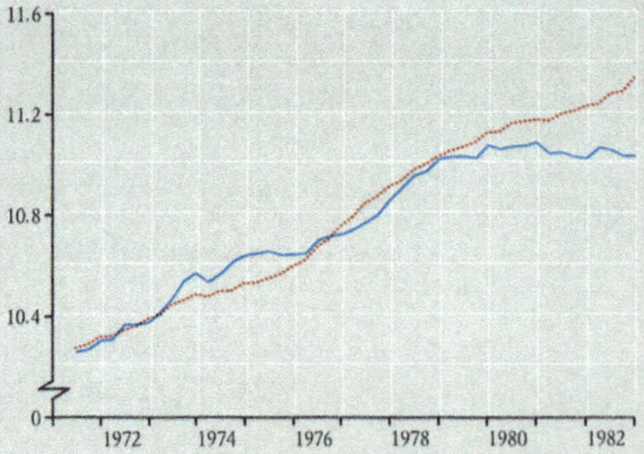

Chart 5.10
Long-term funds raised by the private sector
(billions of guilders)

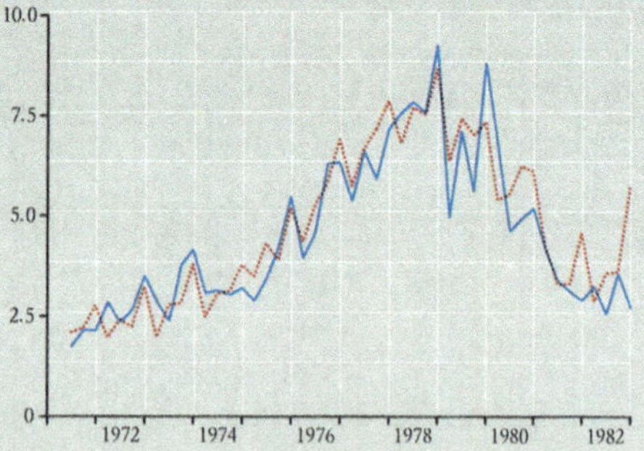

——— historical time path
········ simulated time path

Chart 5.11
Capital market investment of the banks with the private sector
(changes as % of long-term funds raised)

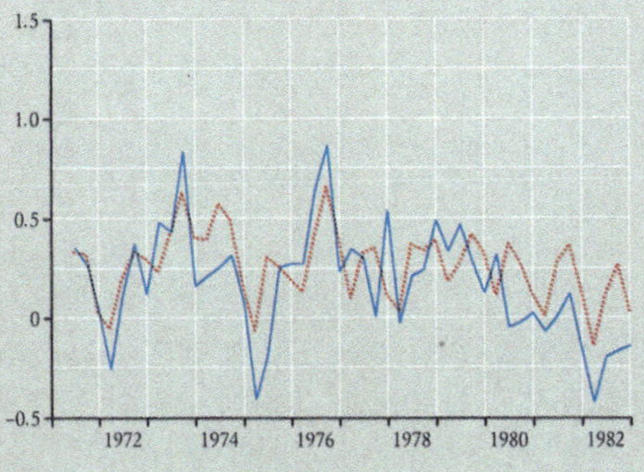

Chart 5.12
Balance sheet total of the institutional investors
(changes in billions of guilders)

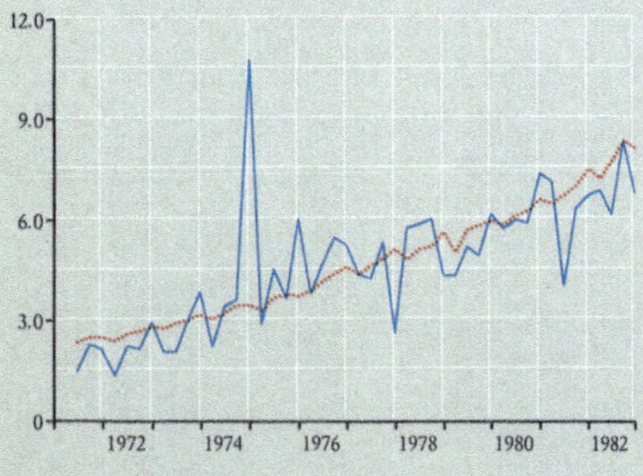

Chart 5.13
Savings deposits with banks
(% of savings deposits)

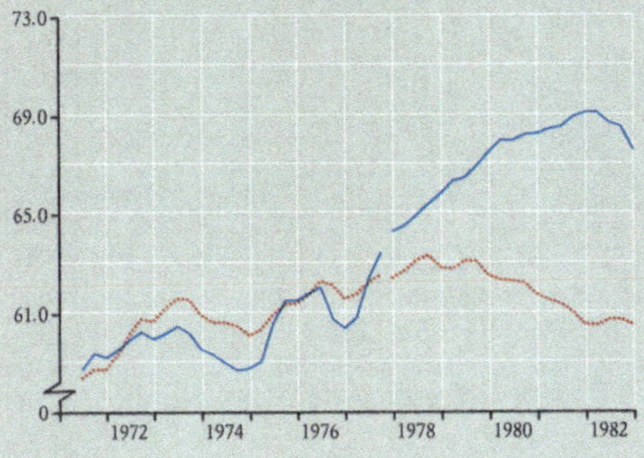

Chart 5.14
Foreign holdings of domestic liabilities
(changes in billions of guilders)

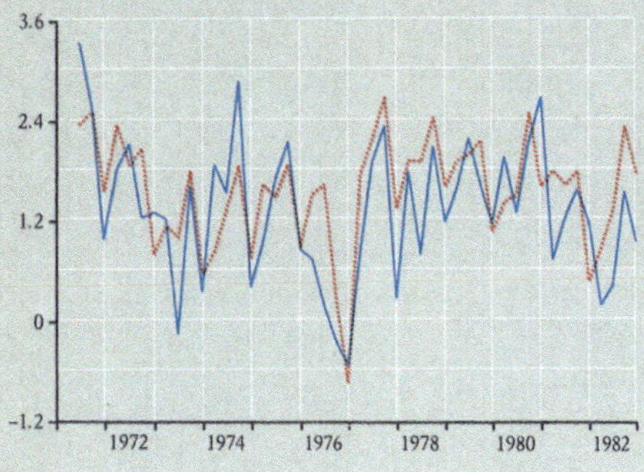

Chart 5.15
Net foreign assets of the banks
(billions of guilders)

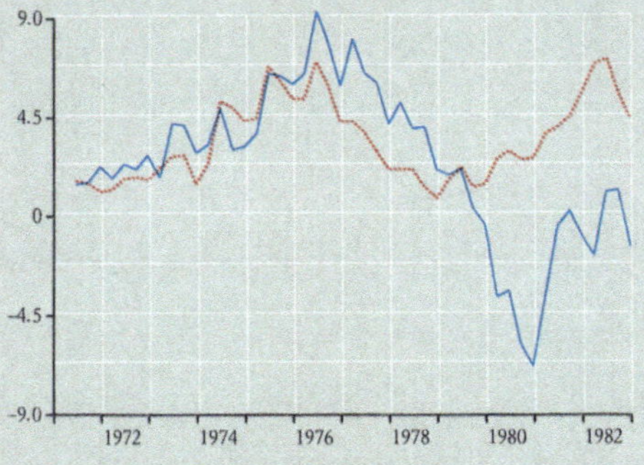

Chart 5.16
External trade credit received
(changes as % of imports)

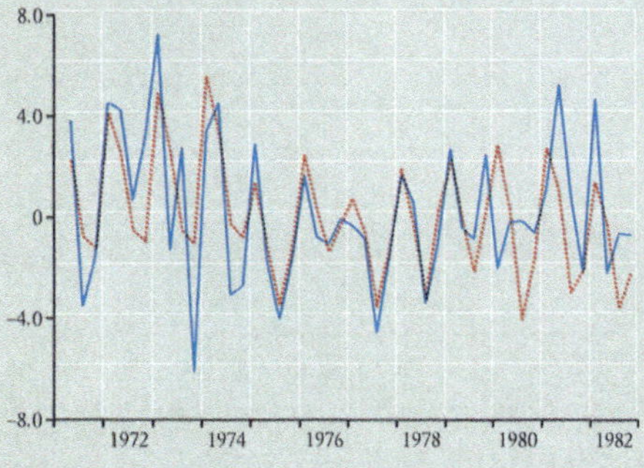

——— historical time path
········· simulated time path

Chart 5.17
External trade credit granted
(changes as % of exports)

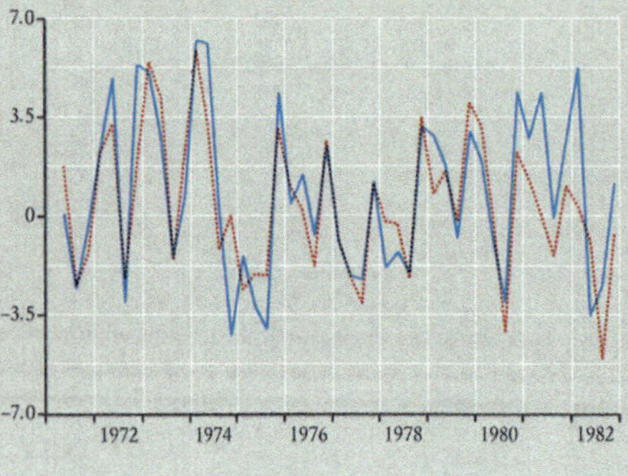

Chart 5.18
Short-term interest rate
(%)

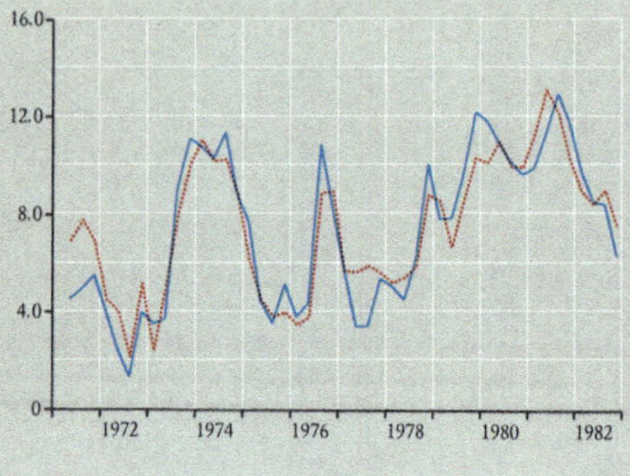

Chart 5.19
Long-term interest rate
(%)

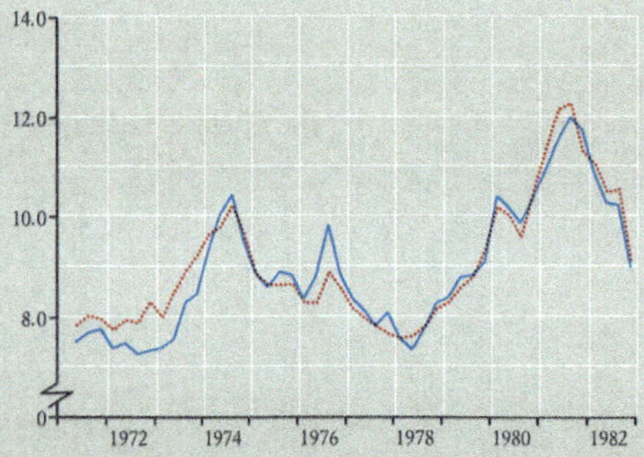

Chart 5.20
Interest rate on current-account balances
(%)

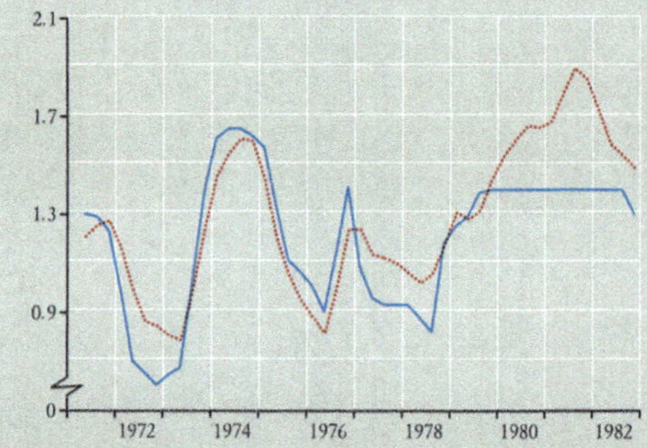

Chart 5.21
Interest rate on savings deposits
(%)

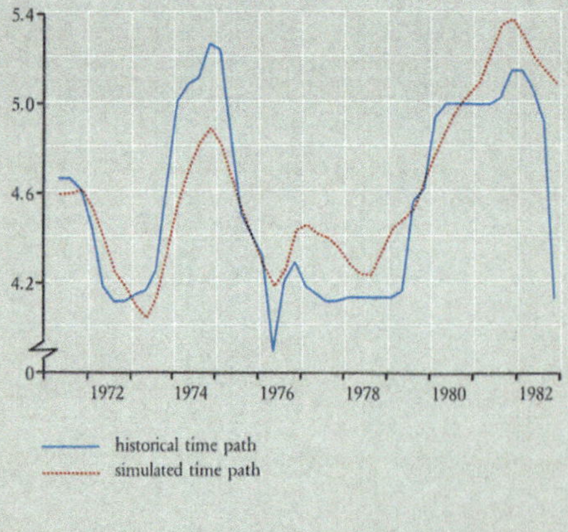

Chart 5.22
Interest rate on three-month Treasury paper
(%)

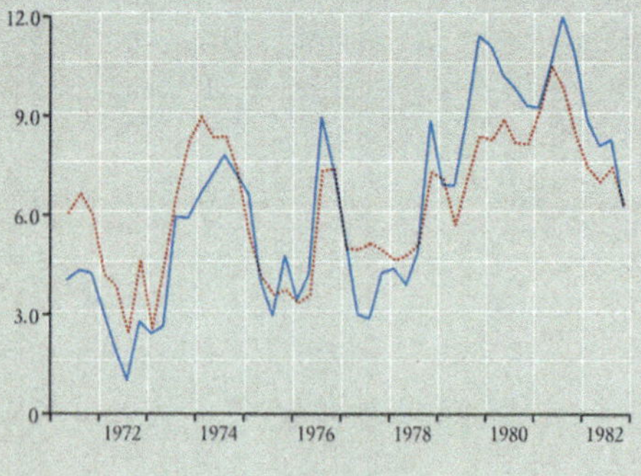

Chart 5.23
Interest rate on short-term bank loans
(%)

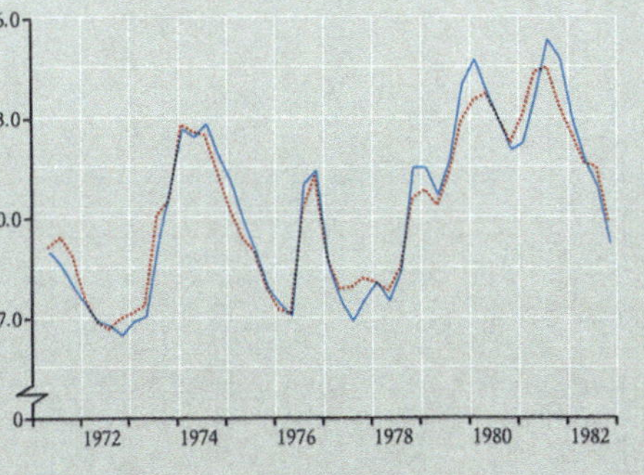

Chart 5.24
Average interest rate on government debt
(%)

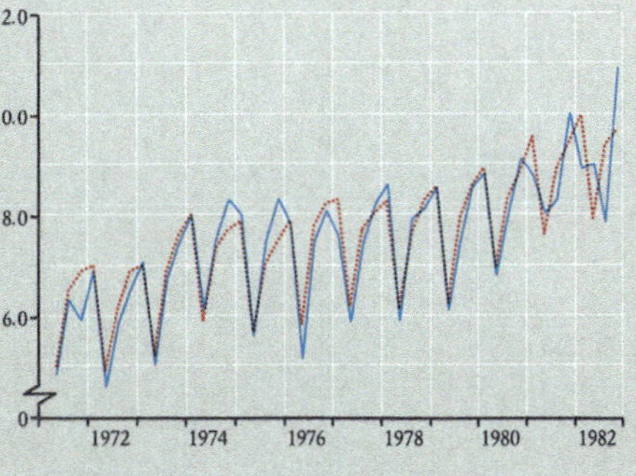

Chart 5.25
Exchange rate of the dollar against the guilder
(% change per quarter)

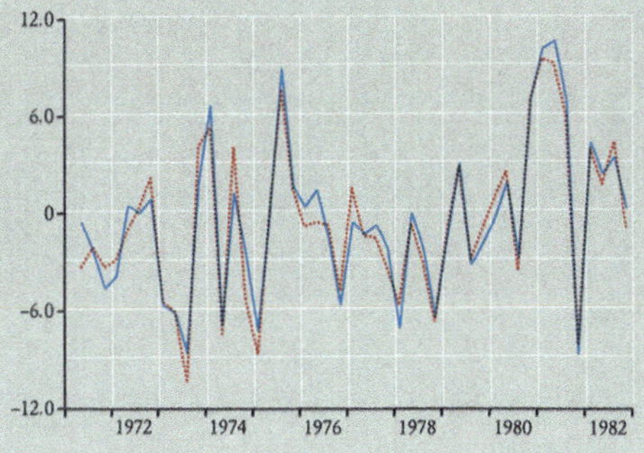

Chart 5.26
Private consumption
(billions of guilders, 1977 prices)

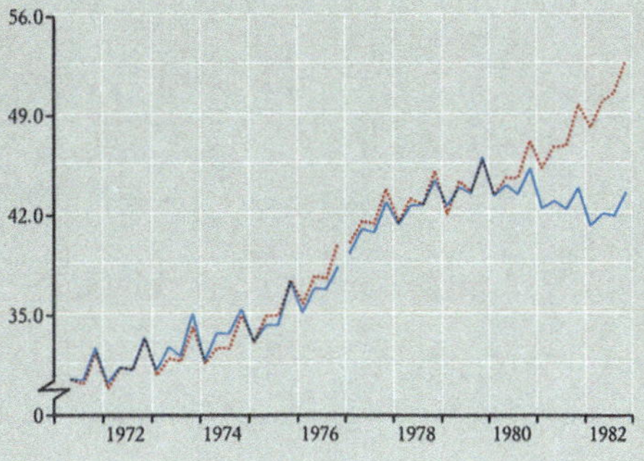

Chart 5.27
Other gross fixed investment
(billions of guilders, 1977 prices)

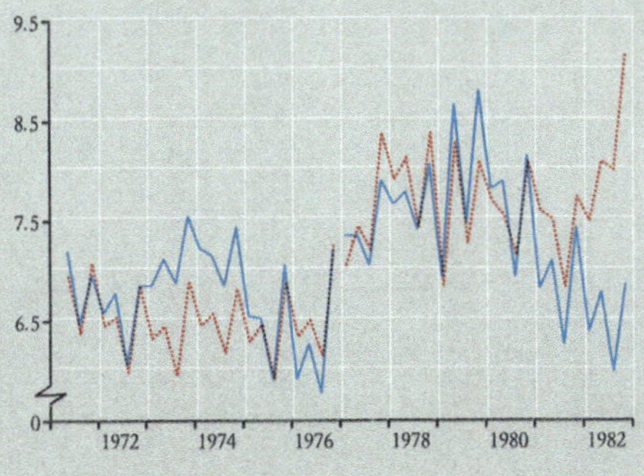

Chart 5.28
Gross investment in dwellings
(billions of guilders, 1977 prices)

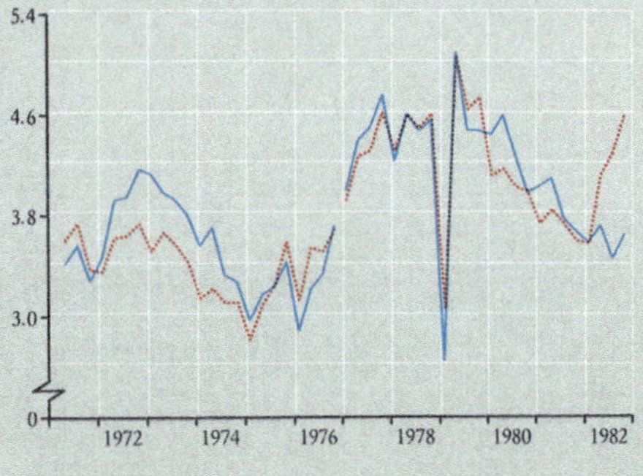

——— historical time path
.... simulated time path

Chart 5.29
Exports of goods
(nat. log. of millions of guilders in 1977 prices)

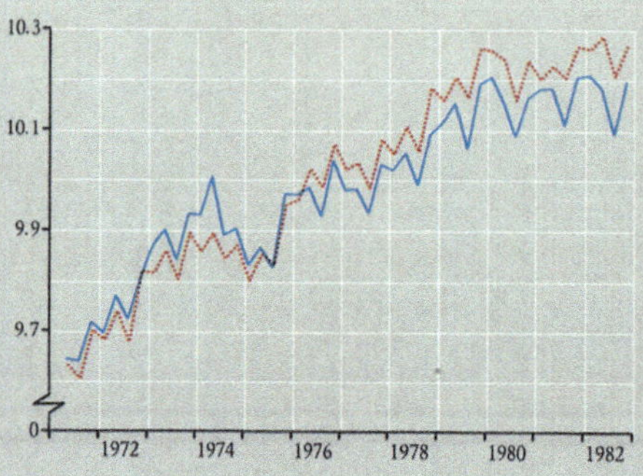

Chart 5.30
Imports of goods
(nat. log. of millions of guilders in 1977 prices)

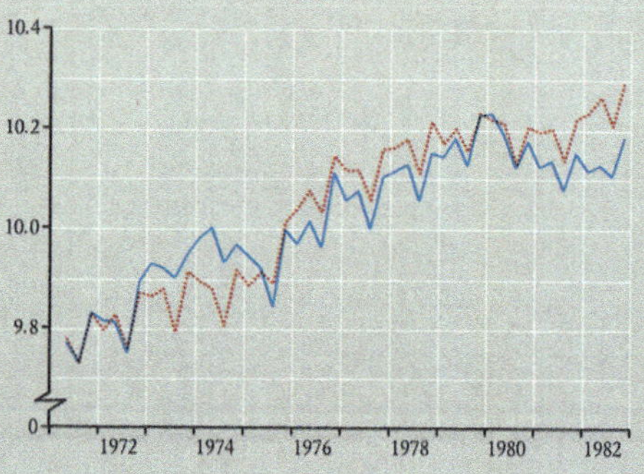

Chart 5.31
Gross output of enterprises
(billions of guilders, 1977 prices)

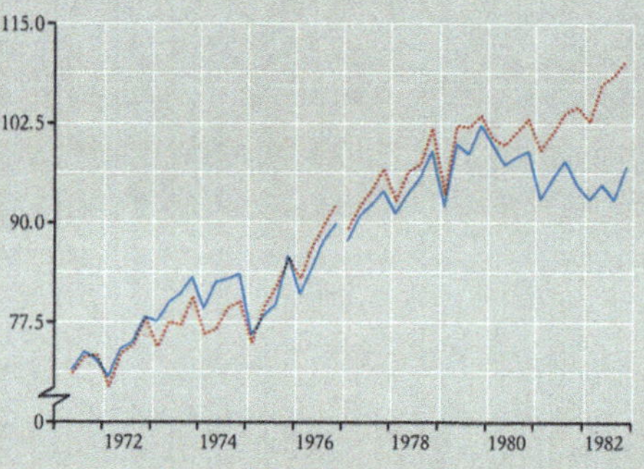

Chart 5.32
Employment in enterprises
(thousands of man-years)

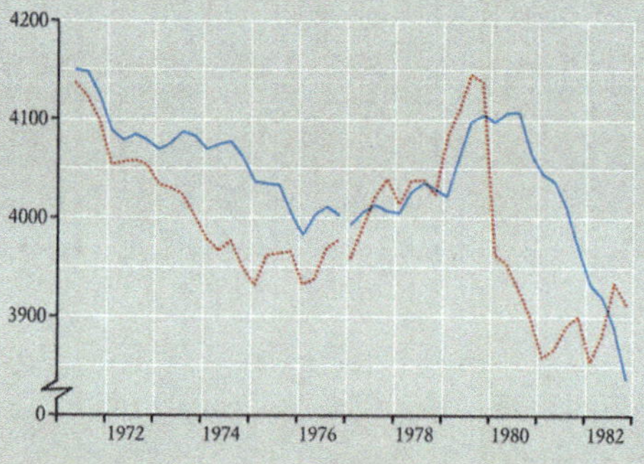

Chart 5.33
Supply of labour
(thousands of man-years)

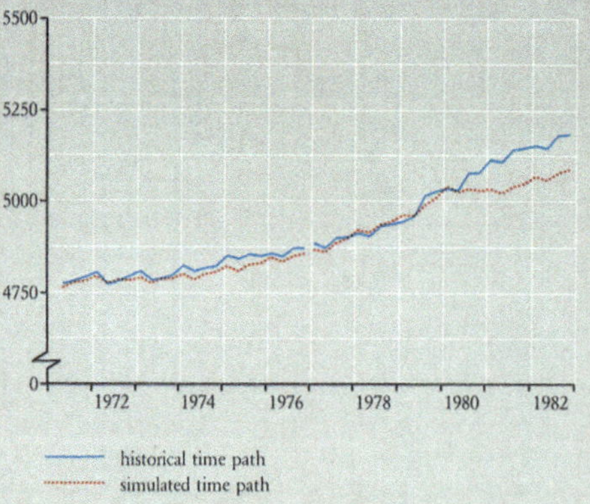

Chart 5.34
Wage and salary bill per worker in enterprises
(nat. log. of amounts in thousands of guilders)

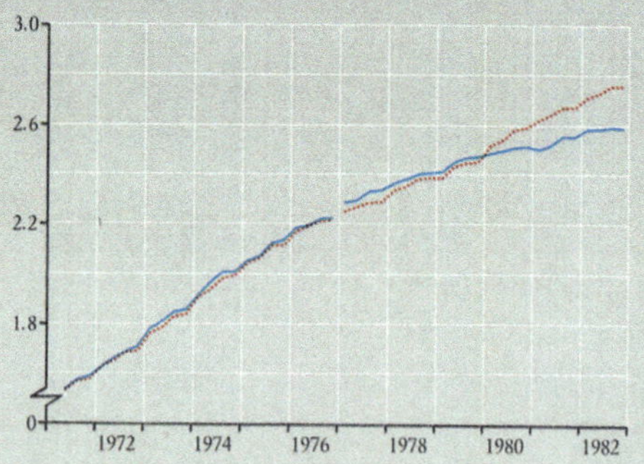

Chart 5.35
Wage and salary bill per public servant
(% change per quarter)

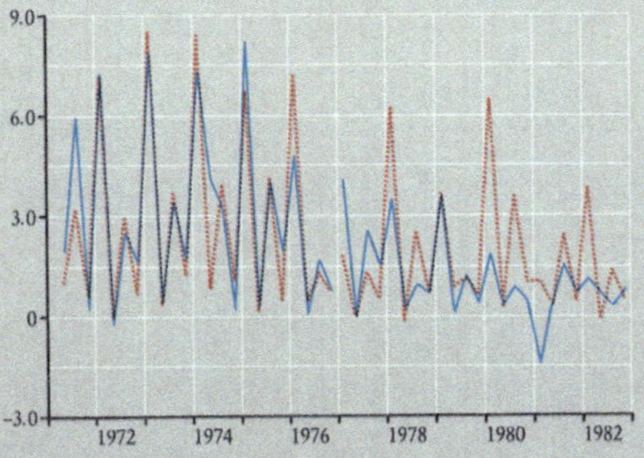

Chart 5.36
Price index of private consumption
(% change per quarter)

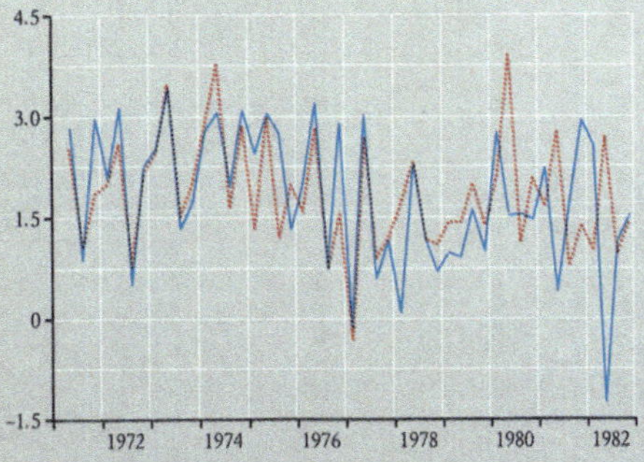

Chart 5.37
Price index of other gross fixed investment
(% change per quarter)

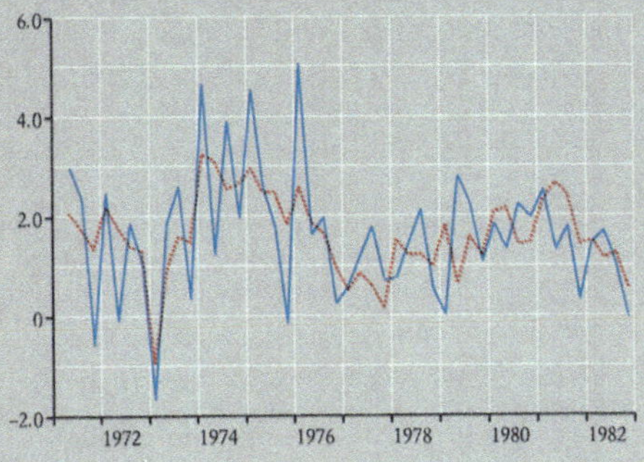

Chart 5.38
Price index of exports of goods
(% change per quarter)

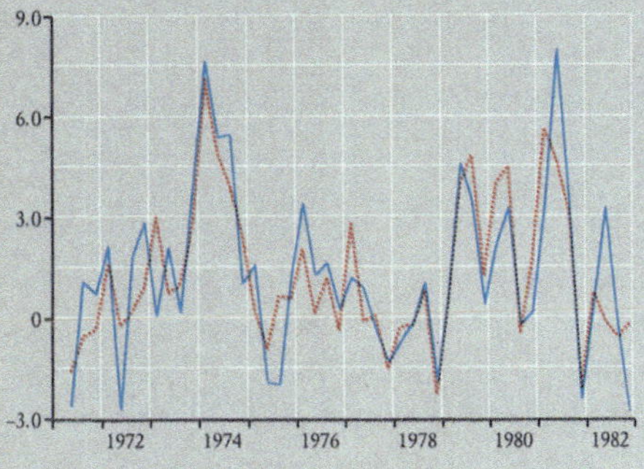

Chart 5.39
Price index of autonomous expenditure
(% change per quarter)

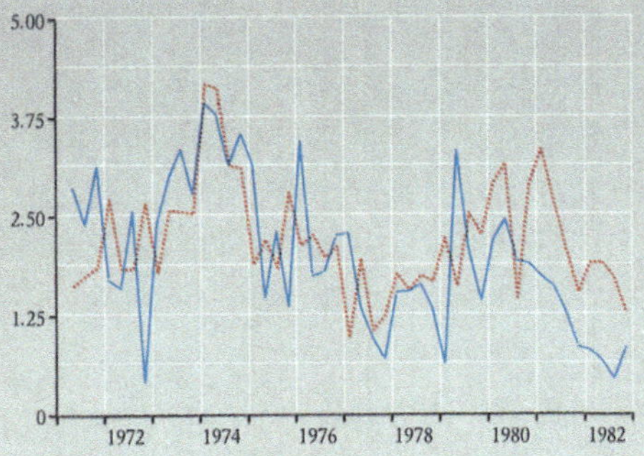

Chart 5.40
Price index of investment in dwellings
(% change per quarter)

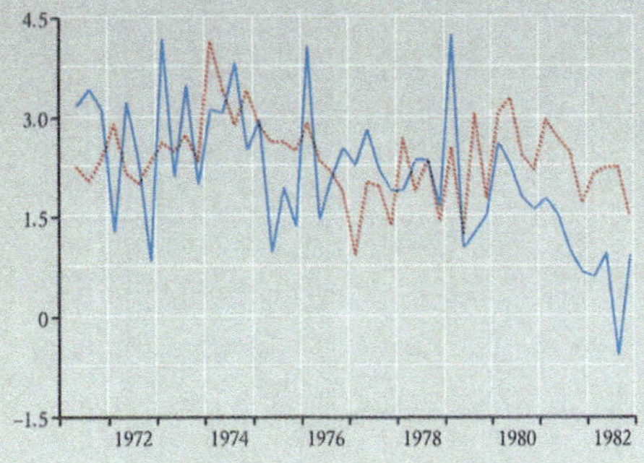

historical time path
simulated time path

Chart 5.41
Price index of stockbuilding
(% change per quarter)

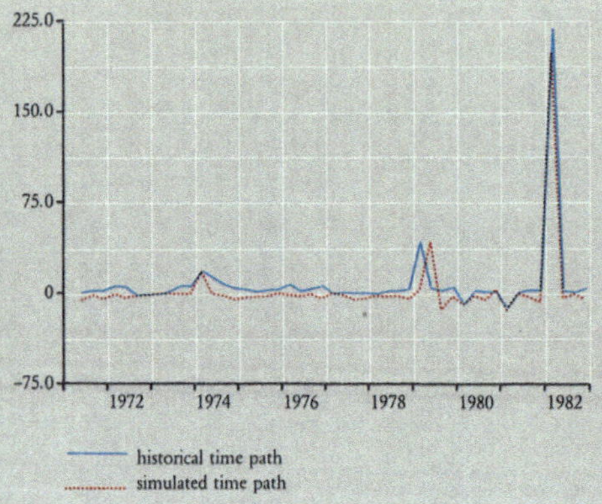

Chart 5.42
Unemployed persons under the Unemployment Act
(thousands of man-years)

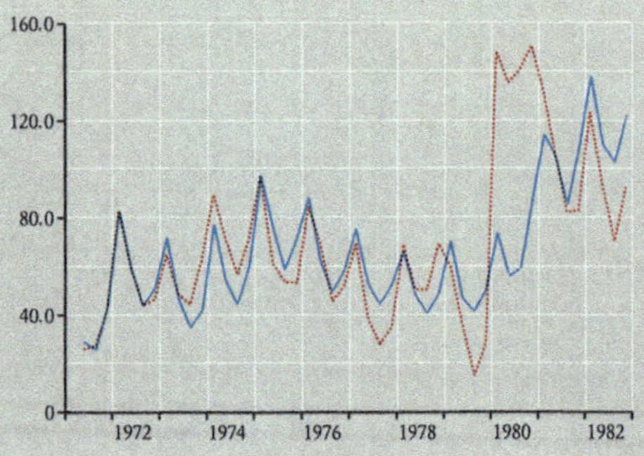

6 The model as a tool for policy analysis

6.1 Introduction

Among the uses to which a macro-economic model may be put is policy analysis. In this respect, macro-economic policy analysis is often – wrongly – viewed as a special achievement of model building. But reality is that any economist advising upon policy forms certain opinions about the consequences of proposed measures enabling him to advise either for or against. He bases these opinions either on verbal or on quantitative macro-economic models. Strictly speaking, ideas about economic relationships have thus always played a role in policy judgements. The use of models as referred to here is in conformity with a long-standing tradition, which, since Tinbergen's model of 1936 and the start of the Dutch Central Planning Bureau's modelling activity nearly 40 years ago, has increasingly taken a more explicit quantitative shape.

The model described in the preceding Chapters is used in this Chapter for a number of experiments. Firstly, it is examined to what extent changes in the exogenous variables in MORKMON influence the endogenous variables. In each case, this is done by analyzing the differences between the endogenous variables in the simulation and those in the central projection, which serves as the base line. For this purpose, a time path has been extrapolated from 1984 onwards. As the results of the model are highly conditional upon the assumptions regarding the exogenous variables, this type of exercise is denoted in the literature as *uncertainty variants*. A second type of exercise relates to the effects – according to the model – of changes in the policy stance on the model's endogenous variables. These are the *policy variants*. They are limited to the economic policy instruments included in the model. Finally, it is worth examining the influence on the model's results generated by a change in key parameter values in selected behavioural equations. This sort of exercise meets to some extent the objection which is sometimes encountered that econometric models are only useful if the present is not unduly different from the period for which the model's coefficients were estimated. Phrased differently, if there is any doubt about the stability of a parameter or uncertainty about its value. Such *sensitivity analysis* may be seen as uncertainty variants, albeit of a special kind. One of the constraints of sensitivity analysis is that, even in a small model, parameter values can be varied to a limited extent only, in order to avoid an overwhelming multitude of results. [1]

The sections below discuss a number of examples from each of these three classes of variants in order to show some implications of MORKMON.

---

[1] An example of such an exercise with a small model is presented by Fase and Van Nieuwkerk (1975) in their analysis of the relationship between inflationary expectations and interest rates in the Netherlands.

6.2 Uncertainty variants

The consequences of the following changes from the initial position in the base line projection were analysed:
- an additional 2 % growth of world trade;
- a 10 % depreciation of the dollar;
- a 2 percentage point increase in foreign interest rates.

In each of the projections, the first quarter of 1984 has been taken as the initial situation. Volumes have been invariably expressed in 1977 prices. All results are presented in Tables of the same format, listing the consequences of the assumed variation in the exogenous variable concerned after 1, 4, 8 and 16 quarters. As the Tables are self-evident, their discussion can be brief.

6.2.1 Additional growth of world trade

World trade has been assumed to grow 2 % faster than in the base line projection. The increase relates to visible trade, excluding energy, and, according to the export equation, initially works out for 1984 at an expansion of goods exports of about Fl. 3 billion on an annual basis. The ultimate effects are listed in Table 6.1.

As to the effects, it is noteworthy that, on account of the relevant short-term elasticity of almost one, the additional growth of world trade initially leads to an equally large increase in goods exports. Subsequently, the effect diminishes somewhat. This is due to the slight price competition disadvantage, which results from the increase in exports. The Table also shows that the income effects cause all expenditure categories to increase slightly, leading to improvements in both employment and the rate of capacity utilization. However, the increase in the utilization rate of capital diminishes slightly as time progresses owing to delayed scrapping and the creation of new production capacity due to increased domestic and foreign sales opportunities. The decrease in unemployment effected by this variant leads to a decrease in social insurance benefits. According to the model, this decrease, combined with the increase in tax revenues consequent on the expansion, results in a decrease in the financial deficit of the government of 0.4 percentage point of net national income after four years. As was to be expected, the balance on current account shows an improvement of about Fl. 0.5 billion in the first quarter (or Fl. 2 billion on an annual basis). Because of increasing imports, this improvement diminishes gradually. The computations show no exchange rate effects, while the liquidity ratio exhibits a slight but lasting decrease. In this context, it is interesting to note the high degree of correspondence with the analogous results generated by FREIA [cf. Hasselman *et al.* (1983), Table 5.1, p. 113].

Table 6.1
Effects of an additional 2% growth of world trade

	Effect after			
	1 quarter	4 quarters	8 quarters	16 quarters
Assumption				
Increase in world trade (%)	2.0	2.0	2.0	2.0
Effects				
(%, unless stated otherwise)				
Volume of private consumption	0.3	0.6	0.6	0.3
Volume of investment (excluding dwellings)	0.6	1.8	2.9	1.6
Volume of investment in dwellings	0.2	1.1	1.8	1.6
Volume of exports of goods, excluding energy	2.0	1.8	1.6	1.8
Volume of imports of goods, excluding energy	0.7	1.7	1.8	1.1
Volume of output of enterprises	0.9	1.0	1.0	1.0
Rate of capacity utilization	1.0	0.9	0.7	0.4
Employment in enterprises (thousands of man-years)	1.7	16.8	23.6	26.8
Unemployment (thousands of man-years)	-1.7	-15.3	-18.0	-20.6
Wage and salary bill per worker	0.1	0.1	0.4	0.0
Labour productivity	0.9	0.5	0.4	0.3
Price level of private consumption	-0.1	0.0	0.1	0.0
Labour income ratio	-0.5	-1.0	-0.7	-0.3
Government's financial deficit (% of net national income)	-0.2	-0.4	-0.4	-0.4
Burden of taxes and social insurance contributions (% of net national income)	-0.1	-0.4	-0.3	-0.3
Real disposable income per worker	0.2	0.6	0.7	0.6
Exchange rate of the dollar against the guilder	0.0	0.0	0.0	0.0
Ditto (in guilders)	0.00	0.00	0.00	0.00
Price index of exports of goods, excluding energy	-0.1	0.3	0.3	0.0
Balance on current account, on a transactions basis (% of net national income)	0.5	0.1	0.0	0.3
Ditto (billions of guilders)	0.5	0.1	0.0	0.4
Balance on current account, on a cash basis (% of net national income)	0.3	0.1	0.0	0.3
Net capital transactions of the private sector (% of net national income)	0.1	-0.1	0.0	-0.1
Liquidity ratio (M2 as % of net national income)	0.0	-0.1	-0.2	-0.1
Liquidity creation on behalf of the government (% of M2)	0.0	0.0	0.0	0.0
Ditto (billions of guilders)	0.0	0.0	0.0	0.0
Short-term bank lending (% of M2)	-0.1	0.3	0.2	0.0
Ditto (billions of guilders)	-0.1	0.5	0.3	0.0
Net long-term operations (% of M2)	0.0	-0.2	-0.1	-0.1
Total domestic money creation (% of M2)	-0.1	0.1	0.1	-0.2
Ditto (billions of guilders)	-0.1	0.1	0.1	-0.3
National liquidity surplus (% of M2)	0.3	0.0	0.0	0.1
Ditto (billions of guilders)	0.4	0.0	0.0	0.2
Ditto (% of net national income)	0.4	0.0	0.0	0.2
Short-term interest rate (percentage points)	-0.1	0.0	0.0	-0.1
Long-term interest rate (percentage points)	0.0	0.0	-0.1	-0.1

6.2.2 Depreciation of the dollar

This section considers the consequences of a permanent 10 % depreciation of the dollar against all EMS currencies. Hence, the cross rate between the guilder and the Deutsche mark – the parity – remains unchanged. The effects of the depreciation are summarized in Table 6.2. It might, incidentally, be noted that within the framework of MORKMON the depreciation variant is wholly symmetrical.

The decrease in the dollar's exchange rate is reflected in a fall in guilder import prices of about 3 %. As is shown in Table 6.2, this leads to an increase in imports of 1 % after four quarters. Expressed in guilders, the decrease in the level of export prices is smaller than that in import prices. Yet, on balance, the result is a current-account surplus of about Fl. 0.4 billion, which means that the price effect more than offsets the negative effect in terms of volume. However, a large part of the current-account surplus leaks out through capital transactions, causing the national liquidity surplus to be considerably smaller than the surplus on current account. The liquidity ratio decreases slightly.

In the real economic sector, favourable expenditure effects are evident, leading to an increase in employment. This is in part the result of the favourable effect on the terms of trade, noted before, which leads to a slight increase in real disposable income per worker and a slight increase in other income (i.e. a decrease in the labour income ratio). Consequently, in this exercise the favourable effect on the terms of trade more than offsets the consequences of the worsening of the competitive position.

6.2.3 Increase in foreign interest rates

This variant assumes a permanent increase of 2 percentage points in all foreign interest rates of the model, viz the short and long-term rates in the Federal Republic of Germany and the United States, or their averages. The effects are listed in Table 6.3. Once more, the initial situation is the first quarter of 1984.

Table 6.3 shows that the increase in foreign interest rates feeds through immediately into the domestic short and long-term interest rates and into the guilder's exchange rate against the dollar and the Deutsche mark. The domestic short-term interest rate initially increases somewhat more than foreign interest rates, owing in part to the depreciation of the guilder induced by the increase in interest rates. In time, the current-account surplus constitutes a countervailing force, causing the increase in the domestic short-term interest rate to become equal to the increases in foreign interest rates. No such effect is apparent for the long-term interest rate. In itself, this means a change in the structure of interest rates. The consequent substitutions within the financial assets initially result in a fall in the liquidity ratio and a decrease in net money-creating operations. It is, incidentally, questionable to assume, as has been done here, that no supplementary policy measures would be taken in such a situation.

Table 6.2
Effects of a 10% depreciation of the dollar

	Effect after			
	1 quarter	4 quarters	8 quarters	16 quarters
Assumption				
Exchange rate of the dollar against the guilder (%)	-10.0	-10.0	-10.0	-10.0
Effects				
(%, unless stated otherwise)				
Volume of private consumption	0.3	0.4	0.4	0.5
Volume of investment (excluding dwellings)	0.3	0.9	1.4	1.8
Volume of investment in dwellings	0.6	1.2	1.4	1.7
Volume of exports of goods, excluding energy	-0.1	0.0	0.2	0.3
Volume of imports of goods, excluding energy	0.6	1.0	1.0	1.0
Volume of output of enterprises	0.0	0.1	0.3	0.5
Rate of capacity utilization	-0.1	-0.1	-0.2	-0.2
Employment in enterprises (thousands of man-years)	1.8	8.6	13.6	22.4
Unemployment (thousands of man-years)	-1.8	-8.0	-10.6	-17.4
Wage and salary bill per worker	0.0	-0.2	-0.6	-0.8
Labour productivity	-0.1	-0.1	-0.1	-0.1
Price level of private consumption	-0.2	-0.3	-0.4	-0.5
Labour income ratio	-0.5	-1.0	-1.1	-1.2
Government's financial deficit (% of net national income)	0.0	-0.1	-0.2	-0.3
Burden of taxes and social insurance contributions (% of net national income)	-0.0	-0.4	-0.4	-0.5
Real disposable income per worker	0.2	0.3	0.2	0.3
Exchange rate of the dollar against the guilder	-9.9	-10.0	-10.0	-10.0
Ditto (in guilders)	-0.28	-0.28	-0.29	-0.30
Price index of exports of goods, excluding energy	-0.7	-1.1	-1.3	-1.4
Balance on current account, on a transactions basis (% of net national income)	0.2	0.2	0.3	0.3
Ditto (billions of guilders)	0.2	0.2	0.3	0.4
Balance on current account, on a cash basis (% of net national income)	0.4	0.2	0.3	0.3
Net capital transactions of the private sector (% of net national income)	-0.2	-0.1	-0.1	-0.2
Liquidity ratio (M2 as % of net national income)	0.0	-0.1	-0.1	-0.1
Liquidity creation on behalf of the government (% of M2)	0.0	0.0	0.0	0.0
Ditto (billions of guilders)	0.0	0.0	0.0	0.0
Short-term bank lending (% of M2)	-0.4	0.1	0.1	0.1
Ditto (billions of guilders)	-0.6	0.2	0.1	0.2
Net long-term operations operations (% of M2)	0.3	-0.1	-0.1	-0.1
Total domestic money creation (% of M2)	-0.1	0.0	0.0	0.0
Ditto (billions of guilders)	-0.1	0.0	0.0	0.0
National liquidity surplus (% of M2)	0.1	0.1	0.1	0.1
Ditto (billions of guilders)	0.2	0.1	0.1	0.2
Ditto (% of net national income)	0.3	0.1	0.1	0.2
Short-term interest rate (percentage points)	-0.1	0.1	-0.1	-0.1
Long-term interest rate (percentage points)	-0.2	0.0	0.0	0.0

In the real economic sector, the effects of the higher foreign interest rates are unfavourable: expenditure decreases compared with the base line projection and unemployment increases. However, after four years private consumption shows a turnround owing to the wealth effects ensuing from the persistent surpluses on current account. The increase in interest charges and the decrease in tax revenues owing to unfavourable effects on expenditure and income cause an increase in the financial deficit of the government of 0.7-1.0 % of net national income.

6.3 Some policy variants

This section discusses two variants of monetary policy and one of wages policy. The monetary policy variants are:

- an increase in the domestic discount rate of 1 percentage point;
- a limitation of the banks' net money-creating operations by Fl. 2 billion.

The wages policy variant is:

- a shift in social insurance contributions from employers to employees.

In the same way as for the uncertainty variants, the first quarter of 1984 has been taken as the initial situation. The results are presented as differences from the central projection and are shown in Tables of almost the same format as the preceding Tables in this Chapter. The variables in terms of volume are expressed in 1977 prices.

6.3.1 Increase in the domestic discount rate

The classical instrument of monetary policy is a change in the discount rate. To illustrate the operation of this policy instrument within the framework of MORKMON, a permanent 1 percentage point increase in the discount rate has been assumed. Furthermore, it has been assumed that this increase is in line with market conditions. Consequently, the increase in the discount rate is accompanied by a 1 percentage point increase in domestic short and long-term interest rates. The results of the model are summarized in Table 6.4.

As expected, the increase in the discount rate thus shaped is reflected especially in the short and long-term interest rates and, through an increase in the interest rate on short-term bank loans (not shown in Table 6.4), in a small decrease in short-term lending, albeit with a slight lag. Fixed investment and investment in dwellings undergo a distinct fall, with investment in dwellings decreasing more sharply than other fixed investment. Net long-term operations (as % of M2) decrease slightly. The liquidity ratio initially goes up to some extent, but decreases somewhat in the longer run. The latter is caused by the conversion of savings deposits into time deposits carrying a somewhat higher rate of interest due to the increase in the short-term interest rate. If, instead of M2, M1 is taken, it proves – wholly as expected – to decrease by over Fl. 1

Table 6.3
Effects of a 2 percentage point increase in foreign interest rates

	Effect after			
	1 quarter	4 quarters	8 quarters	16 quarters
Assumptions				
(percentage points)				
Average foreign long-term interest rate	2.0	2.0	2.0	2.0
Short-term interest rate in the Federal Republic of Germany	2.0	2.0	2.0	2.0
Short-term interest rate in the United States	2.0	2.0	2.0	2.0
Long-term interest rate in the Federal Republic of Germany	2.0	2.0	2.0	2.0
Long-term interest rate in the United States	2.0	2.0	2.0	2.0
Effects				
(%, unless stated otherwise)				
Volume of private consumption	-0.7	-0.8	-0.7	0.9
Volume of investment (excluding dwellings)	-1.9	-8.4	-8.7	-3.6
Volume of investment in dwellings	-3.8	-11.5	-13.6	-11.6
Volume of exports of goods, excluding energy	0.0	-1.4	-1.4	-2.3
Volume of imports of goods, excluding energy	-0.6	-2.8	-3.2	-0.6
Volume of output of enterprises	-0.6	-2.0	-1.9	-1.5
Rate of capacity utilization	-0.6	-1.9	-1.1	0.0
Employment in enterprises (thousands of man-years)	-2.3	-23.1	-51.1	-53.5
Unemployment (thousands of man-years)	2.3	21.8	40.9	41.3
Wage and salary bill per worker	-0.1	0.1	-0.7	0.6
Labour productivity	-0.5	-1.4	-0.6	-0.1
Price level of private consumption	0.1	0.3	-0.2	0.3
Labour income ratio	0.4	1.4	0.5	-0.7
Government's financial deficit (% of net national income)	0.3	0.7	1.0	1.1
Burden of taxes and social insurance contributions (% of net national income)	0.1	0.6	0.6	0.3
Real disposable income per worker	-0.3	-0.9	-1.7	-0.9
Exchange rate of the dollar against the guilder	1.1	1.3	1.5	1.6
Ditto (in guilders)	0.03	0.04	0.05	0.05
Price index of exports of goods, excluding energy	0.3	2.0	1.5	2.4
Balance on current account, on a transactions basis (% of net national income)	0.2	1.4	1.4	0.1
Ditto (billions of guilders)	0.1	1.2	1.3	0.2
Balance on current account, on a cash basis (% of net national income)	0.4	1.4	1.4	0.1
Net capital transactions of the private sector (% of net national income)	-1.8	-0.7	-0.1	0.1
Liquidity ratio (M2 as % of net national income)	-0.3	-0.2	0.7	0.1
Liquidity creation on behalf of the government (% of M2)	0.0	0.0	0.1	0.1
Ditto (billions of guilders)	0.0	0.0	0.1	0.1
Short-term bank lending (% of M2)	0.5	-0.5	-0.3	0.3
Ditto (billions of guilders)	0.6	-0.7	-0.4	0.4
Net long-term operations (% of M2)	-0.5	0.3	0.0	-0.2
Total domestic money cration (% of M2)	0,0	-0,2	-0,3	0,1
Ditto (billions of guilders)	0.0	-0.2	-0.4	0.1
National liquidity surplus (% of M2)	-0.9	0.4	0.8	0.1
Ditto (billions of guilders)	-1.2	0.6	1.2	0.2
Ditto (% of net national income)	-1.2	0.7	1.2	0.2
Short-term interest rate (percentage points)	2.5	2.2	2.1	1.9
Long-term interest rate (percentage points)	1.6	1.4	1.5	1.5

billion in the first quarter. This decrease intensifies to Fl. 2.2 billion after 8 quarters, diminishing in the longer run to nearly Fl. 2 billion. According to MORKMON, an increase in the discount rate leads to immediate monetary tightening, measured by M1. This is not unexpected and by no means implies that, measured by M2, this form of monetary policy would be ineffective. Incidentally, in the present situation in the Netherlands, the discount rate is notably an instrument of 'narrow' monetary policy, which is aimed at the foreign exchange market, rather than of 'broad' monetary policy, which seeks to control the money stock.

To the extent that the increase in the discount rate leads to lower expenditure, as was noticed earlier, this effect is strongest for investment in dwellings and other fixed investment. The adverse effects on expenditure are, incidentally, mitigated by the favourable wealth effects and the appreciation of the guilder, which results in lower import prices.

6.3.2 Limitation of net money-creating operations

A possible implementation of quantitative monetary policy is limiting the banking system's net money-creating operations. In this exercise, this takes the form of a permanent reduction of short-term bank lending to the private sector by Fl. 2 billion. The results, according to MORKMON, of such a credit restriction policy are presented in Table 6.5.

The Table shows that this policy results in a decrease in domestic money creation and in the liquidity ratio. In the real economic sector, a very slight effect on expenditure ensues, which is negative with respect to investment in dwellings but positive with respect to gross fixed investment of enterprises (excl. dwellings). The usual aim of this policy is indeed achieved, as reflected in a decrease in the liquidity ratio of over 0.5 percentage point. The effects on interest rates are slight, while a restrictive policy of this magnitude is insufficient to have a discernible effect on the rate of inflation.

6.3.3 Shift in social insurance contributions from employers to employees

A characteristic feature of modern economies is the increasingly unfavourable price relationship between the production factors labour and capital. It is possible to conceive of several policy variants to influence this price ratio. One of these is a decrease in social insurance contributions payable by employers, which roughly amount to some 20 % of the wage and salary bill and of average gross wages. The variant considered here involves a shift in social insurance contributions from employers to employees to an amount equal to 1 % of net national income in 1984. This means a decrease in employers' contributions of about 2 percentage points and a corresponding increase in employees' contributions. Consequently, this measure is a redistribu-

Table 6.4
Effects of a 1 percentage point increase in the discount rate

	Effect after			
	1 quarter	4 quarters	8 quarters	16 quarters
Assumptions				
(percentage points)				
Discount rate on promissory notes	1.0	1.0	1.0	1.0
Short-term interest rate	1.0	1.0	1.0	1.0
Long-term interest rate	1.0	1.0	1.0	1.0
Effects				
(%, unless stated otherwise)				
Volume of private consumption	-0.3	-0.3	-0.4	0.5
Volume of investment (excluding dwellings)	-1.0	-3.9	-4.6	-2.1
Volume of investment in dwellings	-2.3	-6.6	-7.8	-7.4
Volume of exports of goods, excluding energy	0.0	-0.9	-0.9	-1.3
Volume of imports of goods, excluding energy	-0.2	-1.4	-1.7	-0.5
Volume of output of enterprises	-0.4	-1.1	-1.1	-0.9
Rate of capacity utilization	-0.4	-1.1	-0.8	-0.1
Employment in enterprises (thousands of man-years)	-1.0	-10.5	-24.2	-29.0
Unemployment (thousands of man-years)	1.0	9.9	19.4	22.3
Wage and salary bill per worker	-0.1	0.0	-0.6	0.1
Labour productivity	-0.3	-0.8	-0.4	-0.1
Price level of private consumption	0.0	0.0	-0.3	0.1
Labour income ratio	0.2	0.6	0.1	-0.6
Government's financial deficit (% of net national income)	0.2	0.3	0.5	0.6
Burden of taxes and social insurance contributions				
(% of net national income)	0.0	0.3	0.2	0.1
Real disposable income per worker	-0.1	-0.4	-0.9	-0.6
Exchange rate of the dollar against the guilder	-0.1	-0.2	-0.2	-0.3
Ditto (in guilders)	0.00	-0.01	-0.01	-0.01
Price index of exports of goods, excluding energy	0.0	0.9	0.6	1.3
Balance on current account, on a transactions basis				
(% of net national income)	0.2	0.8	0.8	0.2
Ditto (billions of guilders)	0.1	0.7	0.8	0.3
Balance on current account, on a cash basis				
(% of net national income)	0.5	0.7	0.8	0.2
Net capital transactions of the private sector				
(% of net national income)	1.0	0.3	0.1	0.2
Liquidity ratio (M2 as % of net national income)	0.1	0.5	0.4	-0.1
Money stock (M1, billions of guilders)	-1.2	-0.1	0.1	0.2
Short-term bank lending (% of M2)	0.2	-0.3	-0.2	0.2
Ditto (billions of guilders)	0.3	-0.4	-0.3	0.3
Net long-term operations (% of M2)	-0.9	-0.3	-0.5	-0.4
Total domestic money creation (% of M2)	-0.6	-0.5	-0.7	-0.2
Ditto (billions of guilders)	-0.8	-0.7	-1.0	-0.3
National liquidity surplus (% of M2)	0.9	0.7	0.6	0.3
Ditto (billions of guilders)	1.3	1.0	0.9	0.5
Ditto (% of net national income)	1.3	1.0	0.8	0.4
Short-term interest rate (percentage points)	0.9	0.7	0.7	0.9
Long-term interest rate (percentage points)	1.0	0.8	0.9	1.0

tion variant, which in the first instance has no consequence for the budget of the government.

The results – according to MORKMON – of this policy measure are listed in Table 6.6. Three of them are especially noteworthy. Firstly, the policy has a favourable effect on employment as a result of delayed scrapping, and the creation of new jobs, partly owing to favourable longer-term effects on investment and exports. To some extent this is a consequence of the improvement in profitability in enterprises, which, in the context of this model, is measured by the complement of the labour income ratio. The volume of output of enterprises and capacity utilization show an improvement and a stabilization, respectively, after some quarters. Secondly, the policy variant results in a decrease of about 1 % in disposable income per worker. The decrease in the volume of private consumption is a closely related effect. Thirdly, and finally, the simulation of this policy indicates a slight decrease in the burden of taxation and social insurance contributions and in the financial deficit of the government. The latter is partly due to the decrease in unemployment and to the effect which the decrease in disposable income per worker has on per capita social security transfers. As expected, the consequences of this redistribution policy for the monetary sector are limited.

6.4 Sensitivity variants

One drawback of model exercises is that often they only consider changes in the instruments incorporated in the model. This does not mean that the policy variants are necessarily restricted to the policy instruments included in the model. Another characteristic is the fact that the model's coefficients are frequently determined historically by what Tinbergen has called the economic structure of a certain period. This by no means implies that in reality the parameters of a model invariably act as natural constants. Parameter constancy is just one of the many hypotheses underlying a macroeconomic model such as MORKMON. In other words, this assumption about the structural parameters, like the uncertainty about the assumed values of the exogenous variables, introduces an element of uncertainty into model-based analysis. To illustrate this, experiments have been conducted – on the analogy of earlier work [cf. e.g. Fase and Van Nieuwkerk (1975)] – with regard to the sensitivity of MORKMON's results to specific parameter values. The experiments concerned the interest rate coefficient in the investment equation for fixed assets, the coefficient of the wealth variable in this equation and in the consumption equation, and – fully on the analogy of Kramer (1979) and Huijser and Kramer (1979) – the elimination of the so-called shift mechanism from the wage equation. Generally, the comparisons below relate to the effects of one of the variants discussed in the preceding section consequent on a change in one of these reaction coefficients.

As to the sensitivity to a doubling of the interest rate parameter in the investment

Table 6.5
Effects of a Fl. 2 billion reduction in the bank's net money-creating operation

	Effect after			
	1 quarter	4 quarters	8 quarters	16 quarters
Assumption				
Short-term bank lending to the private sector (billions of guilders)	-2.0	-2.0	-2.0	-2.0
Effects (%, unless stated otherwise)				
Volume of private consumption	0.0	0.0	0.0	0.1
Volume of investment (excluding dwellings)	0.1	0.0	0.3	1.3
Volume of investment in dwellings	0.0	-0.3	-0.4	0.0
Volume of exports of goods, excluding energy	0.0	0.0	0.0	0.0
Volume of imports of goods, excluding energy	0.0	0.0	-0.1	0.1
Volume of output of enterprises	0.0	0.0	0.0	0.2
Rate of capacity utilization	0.0	0.0	0.0	0.0
Employment in enterprises (thousands of man-years)	0.1	0.4	0.4	7.6
Unemployment (thousands of man-years)	-0.1	-0.3	-0.3	-6.2
Wage and salary bill per worker	0.0	0.0	0.0	-0.1
Labour productivity	0.0	0.0	0.0	0.0
Price level of private consumption	0.0	0.0	0.0	0.0
Labour income ratio	0.0	0.0	0.0	-0.1
Government's financial deficit (% of net national income)	0.0	0.0	0,0	-0.1
Burden of taxes and social insurance contributions (% of net national income)	0.0	0.0	0.0	-0.1
Real disposable income per worker	0.0	0.0	0.0	0.1
Exchange rate of the dollar against the guilder	0.1	0.0	0.0	0.0
Ditto (in guilders)	0.00	0.00	0.00	0.00
Price index of exports of goods, excluding energy	0.0	0.1	0.0	0.0
Balance on current account, on a transactions basis (% of net national income)	0.0	0.0	0.0	-0.1
Ditto (billions of guilders)	0.0	0.0	0.0	-0.1
Balance on current account, on a cash basis (% of net national income)	0.0	0.0	0.0	-0.1
Net capital transactions of the private sector (% of net national income)	0.6	0.2	0.0	0.0
Liquidity ratio (M2 as % of net national income)	-0.2	-0.6	-0.7	-0.5
Liquidity creation on behalf of the government (% of M2)	0.0	0.0	0.0	0.0
Ditto (billions of guilders)	0.0	0.0	0.0	0.0
Short-term bank lending (% of M2)	-1.4	-0.7	-0.3	0.1
Ditto (billions of guilders)	-2.0	-1.0	-0.4	0.2
Net long-term operations (% of M2)	0.4	0.2	0.2	0.1
Total domestic money creation (% of M2)	-1.0	-0.5	-0.1	0.2
Ditto (billions of guilders)	-1.4	-0.5	-0.1	0.3
National liquidity surplus (% of M2)	0.4	0.2	0.0	-0.1
Ditto (billions of guilders)	0.5	0.2	0.0	-0.1
Ditto (% of net national income)	0.5	0.2	0.0	-0.1
Short-term interest rate (percentage points)	0.0	0.0	0.0	0.0
Long-term interest rate (percentage points)	0.0	0.1	0.0	0.0

equation from 15.35 to 30.70, the model shows that in case of the uncertainty variant of a permanent increase of 2 percentage points in all foreign interest rates, this doubling causes the response of investment to be about three times as strong: after 4 quarters investment falls by 22 % instead of the 8 % generated by the original variant. The effect on employment yielded by an increase in foreign interest rates roughly doubles as a result of the simulated doubling of the interest rate parameter value. Similar results are found for disposable income and the financial deficit.

The consequences of a doubling of the parameter value of the wealth variable, V_{ps}, in the consumption equation from 0.048 to 0.096 prove to depend on the way in which the effect on wealth is achieved. If it is effected by a reduction in the financial deficit of 2 % of net national income, corresponding to a change in wealth (V_{ps}) of Fl. 2.5 billion, the consequences of a doubling of the wealth parameter are slight (about −0.1 percentage point in terms of private consumption). If an increase of Fl. 5 billion in exports is chosen as the basis for a change in wealth, the sensitivity to the doubling of the parameter value is much higher, as is evident from Table 6.7. Similar effects are apparent if the corresponding parameter value in the investment equation is doubled. It may be concluded from this exercise that, under certain conditions, the uncertainty about the coefficients of the wealth variables does influence the results yielded by the model, but that in this case the way in which the uncertainty is given shape is of even greater importance.

The sensitivity analysis regarding the shifting of increases in taxes and social insurance contributions has been performed subject to the assumption of an increase in direct taxes (excluding corporation tax) of 1 % of net national income. Table 6.8 shows the consequences of this policy measure for a number of variables, with and without shifting effects. In this and the preceding Table, the standard model refers to the version of MORKMON underlying the variants described in Tables 6.1 to 6.6. This standard model serves as the reference for an assessment of the implications of the elimination of the shifting mechanism. These are presented in the right-hand side of Table 6.8. The conclusion from this is clear: elimination of the shifting mechanism has major consequences for most variables.

6.5 Short and medium term

The Tables with impulse effects given above present both short-term effects and effects after 16 quarters. This might suggest that MORKMON has been designed as a model for the medium term.

The distinction between models for the short term and those for the medium term is primarily based on the fact that medium-term models explicitly model not only the consumption-generating effect of investment, but also its capacity-generating effect. Additionally, the aims of the model user play a role. MORKMON contains elements

Table 6.6
Effects of a shift in social insurance contributions of 1% of net national income from employers to employees

	Effect after			
	1 quarter	4 quarters	8 quarters	16 quarters
Assumption				
Wage and salary bill per worker (%)	-2.2	-2.2	-2.2	-2.2
Effects				
(%, unless stated otherwise)				
Volume of private consumption	-0.8	-0.7	-0.4	-0.4
Volume of investment (excluding dwellings)	-0.6	-0.4	1.5	2.6
Volume of investment in dwellings	0.0	0.0	0.5	1.3
Volume of exports of goods, excluding energy	0.0	0.6	1.2	1.2
Volume of imports of goods, excluding energy	-0.4	-1.1	-0.5	-0.3
Volume of output of enterprises	-0.4	0.3	0.9	1.1
Rate of capacity utilization	-0.7	-0.5	0.0	-0.1
Employment in enterprises (thousands of man-years)	7.2	18.3	31.8	40.9
Unemployment (thousands of man-years)	-7.2	-16.0	-26.2	-31.0
Wage and salary bill per worker	-2.0	-3.0	-3.6	-3.2
Labour productivity	-0.6	-0.2	0.1	0.0
Price level of private consumption	-0.4	-1.3	-1.7	-1.5
Labour income ratio	-1.1	-0.6	-1.5	-1.3
Government's financial deficit on a cash basis (% of net national income)	-0.1	-0.1	-0.5	-0.6
Burden of taxes and social insurance contributions (% of net national income)	-0.3	-0.3	-0.6	-0.6
Real disposable income per worker	-1.4	-1.1	-1.0	-0.7
Exchange rate of the dollar against the guilder	0.0	0.0	0.0	0.0
Ditto (in guilders)	0.00	0.00	0.00	0.00
Price index of exports of goods, excluding energy	0.1	-1.1	-1.2	-1.0
Balance on current account, on a transactions basis (% of net national income)	0.3	0.4	0.3	0.3
Ditto (billions of guilders)	0.2	0.3	0.3	0.3
Balance on current account, on a cash basis (% of net national income)	0.2	0.4	0.3	0.2
Net capital transactions of the private sector (% of net national income)	-0.2	-0.1	0.0	-0.1
Liquidity ratio (M2 as % of net national income)	0.0	0.1	0.1	-0.2
Liquidity creation on behalf of the government (% of M2)	0.0	0.0	0.0	0.0
Ditto (billions of guilders)	0.0	0.0	-0.1	-0.1
Short-term bank lending (% of M2)	-0.1	-0.3	0.1	0.0
Ditto (billions of guilders)	-0.1	-0.4	0.1	0.0
Net long-term operations (% of M2)	-0.2	-0.2	-0.3	-0.3
Total domestic money cration (% of M2)	-0.3	-0.5	-0.2	-0.3
Ditto (billions of guilders)	-0.4	-0.6	-0.3	-0.5
National liquidity surplus (% of M2)	0.0	0.2	0.2	0.1
Ditto (billions of guilders)	0.0	0.3	0.3	0.2
Ditto (% of net national income)	0.0	0.3	0.3	0.2
Short-term interest rate (percentage points)	0.0	-0.1	-0.1	-0.1
Long-term interest rate (percentage points)	0.0	-0.1	-0.1	-0.1

Table 6.7
Effects of a Fl. 5 billion increase in exports

	Standardmodel			
	Effect after			
	1 quarter	4 quarters	8 quarters	16 quarters
Volume of private consumption	2.6	5.6	5.4	2.6
Volume of investment (excluding dwellings)	5.9	17.0	25.5	13.0
Volume of investment in dwellings	1.6	9.7	15.1	12.9
Volume of exports of goods, excluding energy	15.8	13.5	11.4	13.2
Volume of imports of goods, excluding energy	6.0	17.4	16.7	10.1
Volume of output of enterprises	9.6	9.4	9.3	8.8
Rate of capacity utilization	10.3	9.2	6.7	4.2
Employment in enterprises (thousands of man-years)	14.7	155.8	206.0	228.9
Unemployment (thousands of man-years)	-14.7	-143.3	-154.9	-176.8
Wage and salary bill per worker	1.4	1.5	4.2	0.5
Labour productivity	9.2	5.1	3.7	2.6
Price level of private consumption	-0.7	0.2	1.5	-0.1
Labour income ratio	-4.5	-8.5	-4.6	-2.1
Government's financial deficit on a cash basis (% of net national income)	-2.1	-3.4	-3.3	-3.3
Burden of taxes and social insurance contributions (% of net national income)	-1.2	-3.5	-2.5	-2.1
Real disposable income per worker	2.6	5.6	6.7	5.3
Exchange rate of the dollar against the guilder	-0.1	-0.1	-0.2	-0.1
Price index of exports of goods, excluding energy	-1.5	3.5	3.1	0.8
Balance on current account, on a transactions basis (% of net national income)	4.2	0.3	-0.4	2.4
Balance on current account, on a cash basis (% of net national income)	3.0	0.5	-0.4	2.3
Net capital transactions of the private sector (% of net national income)	1.2	-0.9	-0.5	-0.6
Liquidity ratio (M2 as % of net national income)	0.2	-0.6	-1.2	-0.4
Liquidity creation on behalf of the government (% of M2)	-0.1	-0.2	-0.2	-0.2
Short-term bank lending (% of M2)	-0.9	3.3	1.8	-0.2
Net long-term operations (% of M2)	-0.1	-1.3	-0.7	-1.1
Total domestic money creation (% of M2)	-1.1	1.7	0.8	-1.4
National liquidity surplus (% of M2)	2.8	-0.3	-0.6	1.2
Short-term interest rate (percentage points)	-0.6	-0.2	0.0	-0.6
Long-term interest rate (percentage points)	-0.2	-0.4	-0.5	-0.6

Explanatory note:
The standard model is the version of MORKMON underlying the variants described in Tables 6.1 to 6.6.

Amendment of wealth effect in consumption function			
Effect after			
1 quarter	4 quarters	8 quarters	16 quarters
2.5	4.7	3.5	1.5
5.1	14.3	21.5	11.3
1.5	8.6	12.9	11.2
15.8	13.6	11.8	13.5
5.8	16.2	14.6	9.4
9.1	8.5	8.1	8.0
9.8	8.4	5.9	4.1
14.5	147.5	186.8	208.1
-14.5	-135.5	-139.3	-161.2
1.3	1.3	3.6	0.4
8.7	4.6	3.2	2.6
-0.7	0.1	1.2	-0.1
-4.2	-7.4	-3.7	-1.9
-1.9	-3.0	-2.8	-2.9
-1.1	-3.0	-2.1	-1.8
2.4	4.9	5.7	4.6
-0.1	-0.1	-0.1	0.0
-1.4	3.2	2.7	0.8
4.1	0.7	0.4	2.7
2.9	0.7	0.4	2.7
1.1	-1.1	-0.7	-0.8
0.1	-0.3	-0.6	0.0
-0.1	-0.2	-0.2	-0.2
-0.9	3.3	1.5	-0.1
-0.1	-1.3	-0.8	-1.2
-1.1	1.7	0.5	-1.5
2.7	-0.3	-0.2	1.4
-0.6	-0.3	-0.2	-0.7
-0.2	-0.4	-0.4	-0.5

Table 6.8
Effects of an increase in direct taxes of 1% of net national income

	Standardmodel			
	Effect after			
	1 quarter	4 quarters	8 quarters	16 quarters
Volume of private consumption	-0.9	-1.5	-1.6	-1.3
Volume of investment (excluding dwellings)	-0.2	-1.2	-3.0	-2.4
Volume of investment in dwellings	0.0	-0.2	-0.9	-1.1
Volume of exports of goods, excluding energy	0.0	-0.1	-0.2	-0.4
Volume of imports of goods, excluding energy	-0.3	-1.0	-1.1	-0.6
Volume of output of enterprises	-0.5	-1.0	-1.3	-1.3
Rate of capacity utilization	-0.4	-0.4	-0.4	-0.1
Employment in enterprises (thousands of man-years)	-5.1	-26.1	-37.9	-43.2
Unemployment (thousands of man-years)	5.1	23.6	29.6	33.0
Wage and salary bill per worker	0.9	1.5	1.7	1.9
Labour productivity	-0.3	-0.3	-0.3	-0.1
Price level of private consumption	0.3	0.7	0.8	0.9
Labour income ratio	1.0	1.5	1.6	1.2
Government's financial deficit on a cash basis (% of net national income)	-0.8	-0.6	-0.4	-0.4
Burden of taxes and social insurance contributions (% of net national income)	1.3	1.6	1.6	1.3
Real disposable income per worker	-1.8	-2.2	-2.1	-1.8
Exchange rate of the dollar against the guilder	0.0	0.0	0.0	0.0
Price index of exports of goods, excluding energy	0.1	0.1	0.2	0.4
Balance on current account, on a transactions basis (% of net national income)	0.2	0.5	0.6	0.3
Balance on current account, on a cash basis (% of net national income)	0.2	0.5	0.6	0.3
Net capital transactions of the private sector (% of net national income)	0.0	-0.2	-0.2	-0.1
Liquidity ratio (M2 as % of net national income	-0.1	-0.2	-0.3	-0.3
Liquidity creation on behalf of the government (% of M2)	-0.1	0.0	0.0	0.0
Short-term bank lending (% of M2)	0.1	-0.3	-0.2	0.0
Net long-term operations (% of M2)	-0.3	-0.1	-0.1	-0.1
Total domestic money creation (% M2)	-0.3	-0.4	-0.4	-0.1
National liquidity surplus (% of M2)	0.1	0.2	0.2	0.1
Short-term interest rate (percentage points)	0.0	-0.1	-0.1	-0.1
Long-term interest rate (percentage points)	0.0	-0.1	-0.1	0.0

Exclusive the shifting mechanism in the wage equation			
Effect after			
1 quarter	4 quarters	8 quarters	16 quarters
-1.3	-2.0	-1.9	-1.5
-0.4	-1.4	-2.3	-0.8
0.0	-0.2	-0.6	-0.3
0.0	0.2	0.5	0.4
-0.5	-1.6	-1.5	-0.8
-0.7	-0.9	-0.7	-0.6
-0.7	-0.8	-0.5	-0.2
-1.5	-15.9	-19.1	-17.6
1.5	14.7	14.1	13.6
-0.1	-0.3	-0.6	-0.2
-0.6	-0.4	-0.2	-0.1
-0.0	-0.1	-0.3	-0.1
0.5	1.1	0.6	0.3
-0.8	-0.7	-0.7	-0.8
1.1	1.4	1.2	0.9
-2.5	-2.9	-2.8	-2.3
0.0	0.0	0.0	0.0
0.1	-0.5	-0.5	-0.2
0.3	0.7	0.8	0.5
0.3	0.7	0.7	0.4
-0.1	-0.3	-0.2	-0.2
-0.1	-0.2	-0.2	-0.4
-0.1	0.0	0.0	0.0
0.0	-0.4	-0.2	0.0
-0.4	-0.2	-0.3	-0.3
-0.4	-0.7	-0.5	-0.3
0.1	0.3	0.3	0.2
0.0	-0.2	-0.2	-0.1
0.0	-0.1	-0.1	-0.1

of a medium-term model because it explicitly endogenizes production capacity. However, the model focuses primarily on the monetary relationships, the way in which they are influenced and their interaction with the real economic sector. In this view, MORKMON has been developed notably for short-term analysis rather than medium-term analysis, although technically it is suited for the latter. The calculation of the effects after 16 quarters testify to this technical capability. However, the uncertainties brought out by the sensitivity analysis in section 6.4 illustrate that this is not MORKMON's main feature.

7 Concluding remarks

7.1 Criticisms of models for policy planning

From the very start in the 1930s macro-economic model building has been subject to scepticism and often negative criticism. Of historical interest is Keynes' renowned discussion (1939) of Tinbergen's exposition about the application of the regression method to investment, a book which preceded his econometric model for the United States which was published shortly afterwards, likewise under the auspices of the League of Nations. In this mainly methodological essay, which was rightly characterized by Klant (1979, p. 409) as an 'epistolary discussion about econometrics', Keynes held that, owing to a lack of stable relationships among other factors, this form of practising economics would be doomed to failure. Incidentally, Keynes' methodological view which becomes apparent from this discussion that econometricians are concerned not so much with testing economic theories as with estimating assumed relationships, must be regarded as fundamentally correct. In this context it is important to note Patinkin's conclusion (1976, p. 1095) that

> *'the criticisms Keynes presented in this review were leveled not at Tinbergen's ambitious 46-equation model of the United States economy, but at the use of correlation analysis to estimate even a single equation'.*

A present-day variant of this criticism of macro-economic models – which are, incidentally, often wrongly identified with econometrics [cf. e.g. Van der Geest (1983)] – originates from theoreticians such as Barro (1976, 1978), Lucas (1976), and Sargent and Wallace (1975), who defend the theory of rational expectations. These authors hold that, as a result of the manner in which expectations regarding prices, exchange rates, interest rates, etc. are formed, an activist or discretionary economic policy is impossible and, consequently, the models designed to that end are unnecessary and devoid of purpose. In the Netherlands, this view, focused on *inter alia* the analysis of policy variants, was recently defended by Bomhoff (1982, p. 5), who argues (in our translation) that

> *'where it is a matter of forecasting for the somewhat longer term, or of the calculation of the consequences of changes of course in economic policy, the value of the existing large econometric models is absolutely nil'.*

In the light of Keynes' aforementioned methodological criticism, it is worth noticing that Bomhoff regards the usefulness of econometric models to lie in part 'in the testing of hypotheses from economic theory'.

It would appear that discussions about the merits of models will never subside [1], nor will it be possible to banish the recurrent doubts about the contribution of economic science to the resolution of the major everyday economic problems. The relevant discussions indubitably have pedagogic value and frequently lead to a better insight or to more effective methods of analysis. This is true of the criticism of both econometric and purely verbal models. The relevant criticism of the macro-economic models is thus to be viewed as one of the many conceivable specific forms of this general criticism of economic science. As argued earlier [cf. Hennipman (1958) and e.g. Fase (1981b, pp. 5-6)], when viewed in a proper perspective, this criticism proves, especially in regard to the macro-economic models, to result from exaggerated expectations of the models in the event of disappointing actual economic developments rather than from a lack of progress and improvement in methods of analysis. The instrumental view of economic theory as worded by Hennipman (1962) and others, which does not seek to distinguish 'between the theory of economic policy and the rest of economic science', is still topical. In this context, Hennipman writes (p. 68) (in our translation):

> *'... that the services which economic science provides to economic policy consist above all of making available the results of its theoretical and empirical research, together with the methods of reasoning and of analysis it has evolved; among the latter, the decision models for quantitative policy, developed and applied by R. Frisch, J. Tinbergen and others, deserve special mention'.*

This is an unambiguous inducement and assignment for builders of macro-economic models to incorporate, to the best of their ability, all eligible innovations from economic theory and econometrics into their work. The question arises which innovations are eligible and to what extent they are to be found in econometric macro-economic models in general and in MORKMON in particular.

7.2 Model building and theoretical innovation

However valuable and stimulating the views of Lucas and his followers – characterized with some irony by Pen (1984) as the RATEX club – may be for the economic theoretician, they leave the model builder no option but to radically end his work. That would not appear to be a constructive solution furthering the cause of economic policy analysis. In reality, this radical course is, consequently, not taken while, moreover, some defenders of the rational expectations *cum* natural rate of unemployment hypothesis seek to formulate alternative models to investigate the policy implications in more detail and to derive conditions for the assessment of the models [cf. e.g.

---

[1] Cf. the recent series of discussions under the title 'Macro-economische modelbouw in discussie' in Economisch-Statistische Berichten.

Sargent (1976) and Van Loo (1984, p. 128)]. These conditions are still of a strictly theoretical nature. Policy analysis invariably seeks to bridge the gap between theoretical abstraction and manifold reality as effectively as possible. In this respect, econometric macro-economic models serve as aids to thinking and as sources of information. Nevertheless, two aspects of the RATEX school's views deserve serious attention. The first is the insight – also formulated by Keynes – that relationships estimated for the past may lose their validity in the future. The mechanical model user is then left in the dark, but to the discerning user with a sound insight into reality the model design may to a certain extent provide guidance by testing uncertainty variants for the parameters concerned. In the present study this has been done in section 6.4. A second aspect of the RATEX school worth noticing is the manner in which the formation of expectations is included in macro-economic models. Without – as argued elsewhere [cf. Fase (1981b)] – accepting the theory of rational expectations in its extreme form, it must be admitted that the role of expectations has remained underexposed in the usual macro-economic models and, where allowed for, has been incorporated inconsistently. The version of MORKMON presented here likewise does not incorporate a full empirically elaborated treatment of expectations. However, for the exchange rates, among other variables, a first, relatively mechanical effort has been made. Further elaboration of this pure expectation theory is necessary and is of major significance for progress in macro-economic model building for policy analysis.

As to the econometric details, MORKMON has been estimated equation-wise, and in some cases block-wise. As is usual in policy-oriented model building, no advanced simultaneous estimation techniques were employed. Use was only made of ordinary or generalized least squares and seemingly unrelated regression. There are two reasons for this. Firstly, the present research project was aimed primarily at designing a structure for the real economic and monetary relationships in the Netherlands economy. Secondly, there is a more fundamental reason relating to estimation methodology. It is connected with the often unspoken starting point in theoretical econometrics that the 'true' model is assumed to be known. Consequently, in this ideal situation there is absolute certainty about the best specification, and use of the theoretically optimum method of estimation is called for. In the case of MORKMON, the starting point is the recognition of our imperfect knowledge of economic reality, which thus constitutes the obvious justification for a more liberal view as to suitable estimation methods than the orthodox econometrician would prefer.

In this context, the question may arise whether it would not be advisable to apply the so-called misspecification tests as devised by, for instance, Hendry (1979, 1983), Hendry and Richard (1983), Kiviet (1984) and Kloek (1984). Although no effort may be spared to improve the models, emphasis has been placed here on the systematic analysis of the data, using the information provided by economic theory. Nevertheless, as is evident from the test statistics given in Appendix I, a start has been made towards an assessment of the behaviour of the residuals in a more sophisticated manner than that permitted by the Durbin-Watson test [partly on the analogy of earlier work on this subject by Den Butter and Fase (1981)]. For the rest, when estimating MORKMON, economic theory had precedence over statistics in the assessment of the individual equations [cf. e.g. Sandee (1966)].

7.3 Epilogue

When the first version of the monetary model developed at the Bank was published in 1981, its partial nature owing to the absence of a real economic block was rightly stressed. Thanks in part to the Bank's confrontation of quarterly estimates of income and expenditure [cf. De Nederlandsche Bank N.V. (1982)], this gap has now been filled so that MORKMON presents a full-fledged integrated model of the real economic and monetary sectors.

It must be noted that MORKMON's monetary sub-model is not identical with its earlier versions MOKMON-1-81 and MOKMON-1-82 [cf. Fase (1981a, 1984)]. Not only has the sample period been updated to 1983 for a number of behavioural equations, but a number of relationships, such as those for the financial assets and the long-term interest rate, have been modified. Consequently, a number of inadequacies in the first versions has been overcome. These modifications relate first of all to the effect of the financial surpluses or deficits of all sectors, instead of the government's deficit only, on interest rates. Furthermore, in the present version of the model, the aggregate M3 no longer plays an explicit role because the technique of the portfolio behaviour models has been worked out in greater detail than in the earlier versions. Like the two preceding versions of the monetary sub-model, MORKMON is not based on a specific concept of money. Thus the great flexibility in the choice of a monetary aggregate has been preserved.

Appendices

Appendix I. The equations used in the model MORKMON

This Appendix contains the equations of the complete model, grouped under three headings:

A. The monetary block (MOKMON-1-84)

B. The real economic block (REKMON-1-84)

C. The equations to link the monetary and real economic blocks

The model bas been estimated with the aid of quarterly data for estimation periods which sometimes differ per equation dating from the years 1970-1983. The sample period is given for each estimated equation. Furthermore, the t-values of the parameter estimates are shown for each equation, as well as a number of statistics which are listed here for the sake of completeness.

The R^2 adjusted for degrees of freedom, $\overline{R}^2$, is calculated nearly throughout. It is a well-known fact that an $\overline{R}^2$ proves to be much lower for first differences than for levels. That is why the $\overline{R}^2$ gives little information about the quality of the equation. Nevertheless, the $\overline{R}^2$ is shown for reasons of conventionality.

The standard error of the residuals, SR, gives an impression of the mean prediction error in the sample period of the equation concerned. The advantage of this statistic is that it is expressed, in a linear equation, in units of the variable to be explained, and in a log-linear equation, in perunages. This facilitates the economic interpretation of this statistic.

The portmanteau or Box-Pierce test indicated as Q(n) is a misspecification test which checks whether the residuals of a regression equation (or ARIMA-model) still show autocorrelation. The test was introduced by Box and Pierce (1970) and is recommended by Box and Jenkins as a diagnostic test under the name portmanteau test. For this statistic, this Appendix uses the formula adopted by Ljung and Box (1978):

$$Q(n) = T(T+2) \sum_{k=1}^{m} (T-k)^{-1} r_k^2$$

with r_k the k^e calculated autocorrelation, m the number of autocorrelations and T the number of observations. For $T \rightarrow \infty$, this statistic is χ^2_n distributed with $n = m-p-q$ degrees of freedom, p and q being the number of estimated AR or MA parameters.

According to Breusch and Pagan (1980, p.244), it is better, in the case of lagged explanatory variables, to apply a Lagrange-Multiplier test than the Box-Pierce test (and Durbin's h-test). This is corroborated by Kiviet's (1983) Monte Carlo experiments. However, in the equations shown, the test value lies in nearly all cases well within the significance limits; when specifying the equations it has been used as a rough indication only. Furthermore, the Box-Pierce test is usually found in standard software, while the Lagrange-Multiplier test needs more calculations.

Presentation of both the Box-Pierce test and the DW or Durbin's h-test seems rather superfluous. This is, however, no serious disadvantage as the last two statistics only test the presence of first-order autocorrelation. If, in the estimation, account is taken of first (or higher) order autocorrelation, the estimated autocorrelation coefficient $\hat{\varrho}$ is given while the DW or Durbin's h-test is not mentioned.

A. The monetary block (MOKMON - 1 - 84)

Behavioural and other equations

1. Balance sheet equality of the private sector

$$FA = BL + LOG_{ps} + S_{fs} + V_{ps} + \underline{LB}_{lo} + BBIN$$

2. Demand for liquidity

$$\begin{aligned} \Delta M2/FA = & \underset{(6.06)}{-\,0.7572}\, M2_{-1}/FA \underset{(4.44)}{-\,0.6622}\, S_{-1}/FA \underset{(3.66)}{-\,0.3993}\, LK_{ps_{-1}}/FA + \\ & \underset{(5.77)}{+\,0.002499}\, r_{M2} \underset{(4.97)}{-\,0.000553}\, r_s \underset{(0.03)}{-\,0.000020}\, r_l \underset{(3.62)}{-\,0.001926}\, \underline{r}_l^{bu} + \\ & \underset{(5.46)}{+\,0.2435}\, Y_{bnpm} \cdot \alpha_1/FA \underset{(0.20)}{-\,0.0078}\, \Delta cadm \underset{(2.87)}{+\,0.0271}\, q_k - \\ & \underset{(2.64)}{-\,0.4113}\, \Delta BBIN/FA \underset{(3.59)}{+\,0.00576}\, \underline{dumb6} + \\ & \underset{(5.98)}{+\,0.00663}\, \underline{d}_1 \underset{(6.69)}{+\,0.0079}\, \underline{d}_2 \underset{(3.48)}{+\,0.0038}\, \underline{d}_3 \underset{(59.56)}{+\,0.3969} \end{aligned}$$

with: $\alpha_1 = 1.0516$ for 1970:III-1976:IV and $\alpha_1 = 1.0$ since 1977:I
(this also goes for equations 3 to 9)
Estimation period: 1970:III-1982:IV
SR = 0.00320

3. Demand for savings deposits

$$\begin{aligned} \Delta S/FA = & \underset{(3.39)}{-\,0.2642}\, S_{-1}/FA \underset{(1.93)}{-\,0.3241}\, BNIB_{-1}/FA - \\ & \underset{(4.97)}{-\,0.001537}\, r_{M2} \underset{(4.97)}{+\,0.001536}\, r_s \underset{(3.62)}{-\,0.001563}\, r_l \underset{(3.62)}{+\,0.001563}\, \underline{r}_l^{bu} + \end{aligned}$$

$$+\underset{(1.96)}{0.0898}\, Y_{bnpm} \cdot \alpha_1/FA - \underset{(1.18)}{0.0431}\, \Delta cadm - \underset{(5.11)}{0.0337}\, q_k +$$

$$+\underset{(19.49)}{0.0280}\, \Delta BBIN/FA - \underset{(4.91)}{0.00739}\, \underline{dumb6} +$$

$$+\underset{(1.68)}{0.00174}\, \underline{d}_1 + \underset{(0.45)}{0.0005}\, \underline{d}_2 + \underset{(0.25)}{0.0003}\, \underline{d}_3 + \underset{(23.99)}{0.1226}$$

Estimation period: 1970:III-1982:IV
SR = 0.00310

4. Demand for capital market investments

$$\Delta LK_{ps}/FA = -\underset{(1.66)}{0.0914}\, M2_{-1}/FA - \underset{(3.09)}{0.2998}\, LK_{ps_{-1}}/FA - \underset{(0.83)}{0.1363}\, BNIB_{-1}/FA -$$

$$-\underset{(3.04)}{0.000601}\, r_{M2} - \underset{(4.97)}{0.000532}\, r_s + \underset{(6.01)}{0.001921}\, r_l - \underset{(3.61)}{0.000788}\, \underline{r}_l^{bu} -$$

$$-\underset{(8.14)}{0.2815}\, Y_{bnpm} \cdot \alpha_1/FA - \underset{(2.32)}{0.0544}\, \Delta cadm + \underset{(3.64)}{0.0254}\, q_k +$$

$$+\underset{(2.31)}{0.2130}\, \Delta BBIN/FA + \underset{(0.79)}{0.00087}\, \underline{dumb6} -$$

$$-\underset{(5.04)}{0.00345}\, \underline{d}_1 - \underset{(5.32)}{0.0038}\, \underline{d}_2 - \underset{(4.75)}{0.0032}\, \underline{d}_3 + \underset{(41.47)}{0.1971}$$

Estimation period: 1970:III-1982:IV
SR = 0.00214

5. Demand for foreign liabilities

$$\Delta BNIB/FA = -\underset{(1.28)}{0.1513}\, M2_{-1}/FA - \underset{(0.55)}{0.0737}\, S_{-1}/FA - \underset{(3.34)}{0.3009}\, LK_{ps_{-1}}/FA -$$

$$-\underset{(3.88)}{0.5369}\, BNIB_{-1}/FA - \underset{(2.52)}{0.000361}\, r_{M2} - \underset{(4.97)}{0.000451}\, r_s - \underset{(0.98)}{0.000338}\, r_l +$$

$$+ 0.001152\, \underline{r}_{-1}^{bu} - 0.0520\, Y_{bnpm} \cdot \alpha_1/FA + 0.0191\, \Delta cadm -$$
$$(3.62) \qquad (1.77) \qquad (1.06)$$

$$- 0.0188\, q_k + 0.1703\, \Delta BBIN/FA + 0.00077\, \underline{dumb6} -$$
$$(0.39) \qquad (0.23) \qquad (0.85)$$

$$- 0.0049\, \underline{d}_1 - 0.0046\, \underline{d}_2 - 0.0009\, \underline{d}_3 + 0.2834$$
$$(9.30) \qquad (8.22) \qquad (1.78) \qquad (83.97)$$

Estimation period: 1970:III-1982:IV
SR = 0.00150

6. Demand for currency

$$\Delta CH/M2 = - 1.0\, CH_{-1}/M2 - 0.083\, (p_{y_{bnpm}} - p_{y_{bnpm_{-4}}})/p_{y_{bnpm_{-4}}} -$$
$$(-) \qquad (4.72)$$

$$- 0.00083\, r_{TV} + 0.41004\, .\, 10{,}000/M2 +$$
$$(4.72) \qquad (17.82)$$

$$+ 0.14828\, Y_{bnpm} \cdot \alpha_1/M2 - 0.01629\, \underline{dumb6} +$$
$$(6.45) \qquad (8.56)$$

$$+ 0.00056\, \underline{d}_1 + 0.00456\, \underline{d}_2 - 0.00200\, \underline{d}_3 + 0.05144$$
$$(0.27) \qquad (2.21) \qquad (1.17) \qquad (2.91)$$

Estimation period: 1970:III-1982:IV
SR = 0.00515

7. Demand for demand deposits

$$\Delta D/M2 = - 0.84432\, D_{-1}/M2 - 0.15486\, TV_{-1}/M2 - 0.32580\, KOS_{ps_{-1}}/M2 +$$
$$(8.90) \qquad (4.47) \qquad (1.43)$$

$$+ 0.013\, (p_{y_{bnpm}} - p_{y_{bnpm_{-4}}})/p_{y_{bnpm_{-4}}} + 0.00816\, r_d -$$
$$(4.72) \qquad (15.13)$$

$$- 0.00833\, r_{TV} + 0.00030\, r_{sc} - 0.08679\, .\, 10{,}000/M2 +$$
$$(15.84) \qquad (1.15) \qquad (2.04)$$

$$+ 0.42804\, Y_{bnpm} \cdot \alpha_1/M2 - 0.00318\, \underline{dumb6} +$$
(8.88) (0.73)

$$+ 0.02154\, \underline{d}_1 + 0.03963\, \underline{d}_2 + 0.00984\, \underline{d}_3 + 0.14134$$
(4.86) (8.96) (2.74) (3.82)

Estimation period: 1970:III-1982:IV
SR = 0.01184

8. Demand for time and foreign-currency deposits

$$\Delta TV/M2 = - 0.09549\, D_{-1}/M2 - 0.8\, TV_{-1}/M2 - 0.24875\, KOS_{ps_{-1}}/M2 +$$
(1.00) (–) (1.05)

$$+ 0.066\, (p_{y_{bnpm}} - p_{y_{bnpm_{-4}}})/p_{y_{bnpm_{-4}}} - 0.00834\, r_d +$$
(4.72) (15.13)

$$+ 0.00998\, r_{TV} - 0.00098\, r_{sc} - 0.41059 \,.\, 10{,}000/M2 -$$
(11.42) (1.14) (9.17)

$$- 0.53037\, Y_{bnpm} \cdot \alpha_1/M2 + 0.01892\, \underline{dumb6} -$$
(10.46) (4.08)

$$- 0.01973\, \underline{d}_1 - 0.04176\, \underline{d}_2 - 0.01544\, \underline{d}_3 + 0.72917$$
(4.23) (9.01) (4.09) (18.78)

Estimation period: 1970:III-1982:IV
SR = 0.01250

9. Demand for short-term government debt

$$\Delta KOS_{ps}/M2 = - 0.06019\, D_{-1}/M2 - 0.04514\, TV_{-1}/M2 - 0.42544\, KOS_{ps_{-1}}/M2 +$$
(1.17) (1.30) (3.72)

$$+ 0.004\, (p_{y_{bnpm}} - p_{y_{bnpm_{-4}}})/p_{y_{bnpm_{-4}}} + 0.00018\, r_d -$$
(4.72) (15.14)

$$- 0.00082\, r_{TV} + 0.00068\, r_{sc} + 0.08734 \,.\, 10{,}000/M2 -$$
(1.37) (1.13) (4.18)

$$- 0.04595\, Y_{bnpm} \cdot \alpha_1/M2 + 0.00055\, \underline{dumb6} -$$
(1.96) (0.28)

$$- 0.00238\ \underline{d}_1 - 0.00242\ \underline{d}_2 + 0.00761\ \underline{d}_3 + 0.07805$$
(1.11) (1.16) (4.34) (4.47)

Estimation period: 1970:III-1982:IV
SR = 0.00512

10. Demand for short-term bank credit

$$\ln BL/p_{sa} = 0.7930 \ln (BL/p_{sa})_{-1} + 0.5148 \ln (SA_{-1}/p_{sa}) -$$
(12.42) (3.38)

$$- 0.0137 \ln r_{bl} + 0.0385 \ln r_l + 0.0034 \ln (IB/p_{sa})_{-1} -$$
(0.35) (0.49) (0.86)

$$- 0.033\ \underline{d}_1 + 0.015\ \underline{d}_2 - 0.018\ \underline{d}_3 - 3.651$$
(2.00) (1.33) (1.55) (5.14)

Estimation period: 1970:II-1979:IV
$\bar{R}^2$ = 0.99
SR = 0.0180
Q(12) = 10.34
h = 0.40

11. Demand for long-term funds

$$\Delta LOG_{ps} = 0.7555\ IB - 0.0880\ r_l \cdot IB + 0.0176\ r_k \cdot IB +$$
(3.21) (3.47) (2.54)

$$+ 0.0056\ \underline{p}_w \cdot \underline{V}_w + 15{,}642\ A^{g}_{q_{-1}} - 390\ \underline{kr} -$$
(3.89) (3.43) (1.48)

$$- 250.1\ \underline{d}_1 - 1{,}199.5\ \underline{d}_2 - 746.7\ \underline{d}_3 - 13{,}124$$
(0.67) (3.52) (1.84) (3.19)

Estimation period: 1970:II-1979:IV
$\bar{R}^2$ = 0.93
SR = 597.01
Q(12) = 11.25
DW = 2.17

12. Banks' supply of long-term funds

$$\Delta(LK_{b,ps}/LOG_{ps}) = \underset{(1.73)}{0.1852}\ \Delta(BTB/BTOT) + \underset{(3.43)}{0.0005}\ r_k - \underset{(3.34)}{0.0039}\ r_s -$$

$$- \underset{(1.46)}{0.0010}\ \underline{kr} - \underset{(0.94)}{0.0010}\ \underline{d}_1 + \underset{(2.43)}{0.0003}\ \underline{d}_2 + \underset{(2.43)}{0.0023}\ \underline{d}_3 + \underset{(3.49)}{0.0170}$$

Estimation period: 1970:II-1979:IV
$\bar{R}^2 = 0.44$
SR = 0.0020
Q(12) = 9.47
DW = 1.55

13. $LK_{fs,gb} = LOG_{ps} - LK_{b,ps}$

14. $\Delta(BTB|S_{fs}) = \underset{(17.98)}{0.0800}\ Y_{nnpmb}$

Estimation period: 1970:II-1979:IV
$\bar{R}^2 = 0.89$
SR = 1.39
Q(12) = 11.38
DW = 2.04

15. $LK_{gb} = LK_{ps} - LK_{fs,gb}$

16. Balance sheet equality of the money-creating institutions

$$\underline{VR} + NBA_b + BL + KOS_b + LK_b + \underline{DA}_b =$$

$$= D + TV + S_b + LK_{ps,b} + GLR + \underline{KT}_{ro} + \underline{V}_b$$

17. $BTB = \underline{VR} + NBA_b + BL + KOS_b + LK_b + \underline{DA}_b$

18. $BTOT = BTB + S_{fs} + BTB|S_{fs}$

19. Allocation of savings deposits

$$S_b/S = \underset{(34.62)}{0.9413}\ (S_b/S)_{-1} + \underset{(5.24)}{0.0010}\ (r_s - r_k) + \underset{(1.26)}{0.0012}\ \underline{kr} +$$

$$+ \underset{(2.44)}{0.003}\ \underline{d}_1 + \underset{(3.78)}{0.005}\ \underline{d}_2 + \underset{(2.82)}{0.004}\ \underline{d}_3 + \underset{(2.14)}{0.036}$$

Estimation period: 1970:II-1979:IV
$\bar{R}^2 = 0.97$
SR = 0.0030
Q(12) = 15.88
h = 1.75

20. $S_{fs} = S - S_b$

21. Foreign holdings of domestic liabilities

$$\Delta BBIN/MW = \underset{(1.46)}{577.17}\ \Delta(r_l - \underline{r}_l^{bu})_{-1/2} - \underset{(1.20)}{0.1255}\ (B_{-sa} - M_{-sa})/MW -$$

$$- \underset{(2.44)}{0.2539}\ (B_{-sa} - M_{-sa})_{-1}/MW + \underset{(-)}{0.11}\ \Delta VAS/MW -$$

$$- \underset{(1.36)}{194.54}\ \Delta cadm_{-1/2} \cdot 100 - \underset{(3.86)}{1939.60}\ \underline{dumr_k2} +$$

$$+ \underset{(2.20)}{710.25}\ \underline{d}_1 + \underset{(1.76)}{573.53}\ \underline{d}_2 + \underset{(2.87)}{1{,}052.17}\ \underline{d}_3 - \underset{(3.71)}{966.99}$$

Estimation period: 1971:I-1981:IV
$\bar{R}^2 = 0.50$
SR = 645.84
Q(12) = 10.51
DW = 1.85

22. $NBA_{ps} = NBA_{ps_{-1}} + \Delta BNIB - \Delta BBIN$

23. Net foreign assets of banks

$$NBA_b = \underset{(11.27)}{0.8029}\ NBA_{b_{-1}} - \underset{(0.36)}{103}\ (r_l - \underline{r}_l^{bu}) + \underset{(2.30)}{0.4034}\ (B_{-sa} - M_{-sa}) -$$

$$- \underset{(2.12)}{0.6242}\ (\underline{SWAP} - 0.8029\ \underline{SWAP}_{-1}) + \underset{(2.93)}{1.864}\ \underline{dumkwart2} +$$

$$
\begin{array}{llll}
+ 534.2\, \underline{d}_1 & + 583.5\, \underline{d}_2 & + 408.8\, \underline{d}_3 & - 57.2 \\
(1.13) & (1.15) & (0.88) & (0.14)
\end{array}
$$

Estimation period: 1970:II-1979:IV

$\bar{R}^2 = 0.86$

SR = 877.44

Q(12) = 18.71

h = -2.06

24. External trade credit received

$$
\begin{array}{l}
\Delta HKO_{bu}/M_{-sa_{-1}} = \underset{(1.56)}{0.0058}\, \Delta r_{bl} \cdot \underline{dum1975HKO} + \underset{(0.55)}{0.053}\, \Delta M_{-sa}/M_{-sa_{-1}} + \\
+ \underset{(0.79)}{0.0759}\, (\Delta M_{-sa}/M_{-sa_{-1}})_{-1} + \underset{(2.44)}{0.034}\, \underline{d}_1 + \underset{(0.88)}{0.011}\, \underline{d}_2 - \\
- \underset{(1.99)}{0.024}\, \underline{d}_3 + \underset{(1.46)}{0.023}\, \underline{d}_1\, 70/74 + \underset{(1.63)}{0.025}\, \underline{d}_2\, 70/74 + \\
+ \underset{(1.91)}{0.028}\, \underline{d}_3\, 70/74 - \underset{(1.83)}{0.015}
\end{array}
$$

Estimation period: 1970:III-1979:IV

$\bar{R}^2 = 0.48$

SR = 0.0215

Q(12) = 13.79

DW = 2.18

25. External trade credit granted

$$
\begin{array}{l}
\Delta HKV_{bu}/B_{-sa_{-1}} = \underset{(2.26)}{0.0114}\, \Delta r_{bl}^{bu} + \underset{(2.80)}{0.1993}\, \Delta B_{-sa}/B_{-sa_{-1}} + \\
+ \underset{(1.48)}{0.1071}\, (\Delta B_{-sa}/B_{-sa_{-1}})_{-1} - \underset{(0.56)}{0.008}\, \underline{d}_1 - \underset{(1.45)}{0.016}\, \underline{d}_2 - \underset{(2.97)}{0.036}\, \underline{d}_3 + \\
+ \underset{(2.72)}{0.031}\, \underline{d}_1\, 70/74 + \underset{(2.42)}{0.029}\, \underline{d}_2\, 70/74 - \underset{(0.05)}{0.001}\, \underline{d}_3\, 70/74 - \\
- \underset{(1.87)}{0.020}\, \underline{d}_4\, 70/74 + \underset{(0.76)}{0.007}
\end{array}
$$

Estimation period: 1970:III-1979:IV
$\bar{R}^2$ = 0.69
SR = 0.0164
Q(12) = 10.58
DW = 2.45

26. $\Delta HK_{bu} = \Delta HKO_{bu} - \Delta HKV_{bu}$

27. $LR = E + \Delta HK_{bu} + \underline{LRRV}$

28. Short-term interest rate

$$r_k = \underset{(16.62)}{0.9941}\ \underline{r}_k^{DU} + \underset{(2.80)}{43.274}\ cadm + \underset{(6.88)}{3.882}\ \underline{dumr_k} -$$

$$- \underset{(3.63)}{33.407}\ (B_{-sa} - M_{-sa})_{-1/2}/(B_{-sa} + M_{-sa}) + \underset{(3.27)}{1.538}$$

Estimation period: 1973:II-1982:IV
$\bar{R}^2$ = 0.88
SR = 1.01
Q(12) = 11.08
DW = 1.71

29. Long-term interest rate

$$r_l = \underset{(0.70)}{2.192}\ (p_{y_{bnpm}} - p_{y_{bnpm_{-4}}})/p_{y_{bnpm_{-4}}} + \underset{(4.21)}{0.102}\ r_k + \underset{(4.28)}{0.421}\ \underline{r}_l^{DU} +$$

$$+ \underset{(3.36)}{0.281}\ \underline{r}_l^{VS} + \underset{(2.05)}{4.352}\ \hat{e}_{\$} + \underset{(1.55)}{11.039}\ (\sum_{j=0}^{3} DVL'_{-j}/\alpha_2 \cdot \sum_{j=0}^{3} Y_{nnpmb_{-j}}) +$$

$$+ \underset{(0.97)}{1.163}$$

with: $\alpha_2 = 1.0565$ for 1971:II-1976:IV and $\alpha_2 = 1.0$ since 1977:I
Estimation period: 1971:II-1980:IV
$\bar{R}^2$ = 0.93
SR = 0.26
Q(11) = 14.60
$\hat{\varrho}$ = 0.82

30. Interest rate on current-account balances

$$r_d = \underset{(8.28)}{0.5483}\, r_{d_{-1}} + \underset{(8.18)}{0.0601}\, r_{k_{-1/2}} - \underset{(1.48)}{1.1837}\, \Delta D/BTB + \underset{(2.42)}{0.137}$$

Estimation period: 1970:II-1979:IV

$\bar{R}^2$ = 0.92

SR = 0.09

Q(12) = 9.25

h = 0.72

31. Interest rate on savings deposits

$$r_s = \underset{(11.61)}{0.7897}\, r_{s_{-1}} + \underset{(3.98)}{0.0429}\, r_{k_{-1/2}} - \underset{(1.03)}{2.9821}\, \Delta S_b/BTB + \underset{(2.61)}{0.684}$$

Estimation period: 1970:II-1979:IV

$\bar{R}^2$ = 0.88

SR = 0.12

Q(12) = 5.45

h = 0.68

32. Interest rate on three-month Treasury paper

$$r_{sc} = \underset{(17.40)}{0.7398}\, r_k + \underset{(1.16)}{0.709}$$

Estimation period: 1970:II-1979:IV

$\bar{R}^2$ = 0.94

SR = 0.53

Q(11) = 7.55

$\hat{\varrho}$ = 0.84

33. Interest rate on short-term bank loans

$$r_{bl} = \underline{r}_{cb} + \underset{(6.51)}{0.327}\, dumr_{bl} (r_k - \underline{r}_{cb}) + \underset{(5.53)}{0.230}\, (dumr_{bl} (r_k - \underline{r}_{cb}))_{-1} +$$

$$+ \underset{(2.56)}{18.73}\, dumr_{bl} (\Delta BL/BTB)_{-1} - \underset{(4.80)}{1.13}\, \underline{dum1973r}_{bl} + \underset{(59.68)}{2.433}$$

with: $dumr_{bl} = 1$ if $r_k > \underline{r}_{cb}$
$= 0$ in all other cases

Estimation period: 1970:III-1979:III
$\bar{R}^2 = 0.88$
SR $= 0.20$
Q(12) $= 11.03$
DW $= 1.37$

34. Interest rate on time and foreign-currency deposits

$$r_{TV} = r_k$$

35. Interest rate on domestic money stock

$$r_{M2} = (D/M2)r_d + (KOS_{ps}/M2)r_{sc} + (TV/M2)r_{TV}$$

36. Exchange rate of the dollar against the guilder

$$\dot{e}_{\$} = \underset{(-)}{20}\ \Delta\Delta NBA_{cb}/(B_{-sa} + M_{-sa}) - \underset{(2.60)}{0.3487}\ \Delta r_k + \underset{(4.40)}{0.9171}\ \Delta \underline{r}_k^{DU} +$$

$$+ \underset{(1.73)}{0.2162}\ \Delta \underline{r}_k^{VS} + \underset{(19.45)}{0.8474}\ \underline{\dot{e}}_{DM.\$} - \underset{(2.70)}{0.3202}\ \underline{dump}\ (\underline{\dot{p}}_{VS} - \underline{\dot{p}}_{DU}) -$$

$$- \underset{(2.22)}{20.3687}\ \Delta(B_{-sa} - M_{-sa})/(B_{-sa} + M_{-sa}) + \underset{(1.95)}{0.4447}$$

Estimation period: 1970:III-1982:IV
$\bar{R}^2 = 0.91$
SR $= 1.41$
Q(12) $= 15.15$
DW $= 1.86$

37. $\Delta NBA_{cb} = \Delta IR - \Delta \underline{IR}_{aut}$

38. Expected change in exchange rate of the dollar against the guilder

$$\hat{\dot{e}}_{\$} = 0.50\ \dot{e}_{\$} + 0.25\ \dot{e}_{\$_{-1}} + 0.15\ \dot{e}_{\$_{-2}} + 0.10\ \dot{e}_{\$_{-3}}$$

39. Exchange rate of the Deutsche mark against the guilder

$$\dot{e}_{DM} = \dot{e}_{\$} - \underline{\dot{e}}_{DM.\$}$$

40. $cadm = (e_{DM} - \underline{\bar{e}}_{DM})/\underline{\bar{e}}_{DM}$

41. $CH_{cb} = CH - \underline{CH}_{ro}$

42. $\Sigma FT_o^* = \Sigma FT_o + \underline{NBA}_o + \underline{LB}_{lo}$

43. $VAS = VAS_{-1} + \delta_1 \,.\, FT_o^*$

44. $VLS = VLS_{-1} + \delta_2 \,.\, FT_o^*$

45. Balance sheet equality of the government

$$SSCH = SSCH_{-1} + (\delta_1+\delta_2-1)FT_o^*$$

46. $KOS_b = VLS - KOS_{ps} - \underline{KOS}_{cb} - \underline{CH}_{ro} + \underline{KT}_{ro}$

47. Balance-of-payments equality

$$\Delta IR = LR + \underline{RBO} + \underline{NBARV} - \Delta NBA_{ps} - \Delta NBA_b - \Delta \underline{NBA}_o$$

48. $LK_{ps,b} = LK_{gb} - LK_{ps,o}$

49. $LK_{ps,o} = VAS - \underline{LK}_{b,o} - \underline{LK}_{cb,o}$

50. $LK_b = LK_{b,ps} + \underline{LK}_{b,o}$

51. $V_{ps} = \Sigma LR + \Sigma FT_o + \Sigma \underline{NBARV} - \underline{V}_{cb} - \underline{V}_b + \Sigma \underline{RBO} + \underline{DA}_b$

52. Tension in the capital market

$$DVL' = \Delta VAS + \Delta LK_{b,ps} + \Delta LK_{fs,gb} - \Delta LK_{ps,b}$$

B. The real economic block (REKMON – 1 – 84)

Behavioural equations

53. Private consumption

$$c = \underset{(29.20)}{0.841} \sum_{j=0}^{1} \zeta_j (W_d/p_c)_{-j} + \underset{(3.95)}{0.294} \sum_{j=0}^{3} \eta_j (Z_{od}/p_c)_{-j} -$$

$$- \underset{(1.90)}{116.083}\, r_l + \underset{(3.60)}{0.048}\, V_{ps}/p_c + \underset{(1.38)}{105.927}\, \dot{p}_{c_{-1}} + \underset{(4.24)}{1{,}274}\, \underline{dumb1} -$$

$$- \underset{(15.90)}{2{,}664.6}\, \underline{d}_1 - \underset{(10.20)}{1{,}530.6}\, \underline{d}_2 - \underset{(13.03)}{2{,}426.8}\, \underline{d}_3 - \underset{(0.49)}{533.8}$$

with: $\zeta_0 = 0.75$ $\zeta_1 = 0.25$
$\eta_0 = 0.40$ $\eta_1 = 0.30$ $\eta_2 = 0.20$ $\eta_3 = 0.10$

Estimation period: 1970:I-1979:IV
$\bar{R}^2 = 0.99$
SR = 266.05
Q(11) = 10.65
$\hat{\varrho} = -0.28$

54. Other gross fixed investment

$$i_{-sa} = \underset{(2.12)}{0.285}\, i_{-sa_{-1}} - \underset{(1.76)}{15.351} \left(1/4 \sum_{j=0}^{3} r_{l_{-j}}^2\right) + \underset{(2.93)}{0.331} \left(1/4 \sum_{j=2}^{5} (Z_{od}/p_{y_{bm}} + \underline{f}_b)_{-j}\right) +$$

$$+ \underset{(1.69)}{11{,}658.386} \left(1/4 \sum_{j=0}^{3} (LQ - 1/8 \sum_{i=0}^{7} LQ_{-i})_{-j}\right) - \underset{(1.90)}{728.694}\, (BL + LOG_{ps})/Y_{nnpm} +$$

$$+ \underset{(1.38)}{2{,}959.099}\, q_k - \underset{(1.87)}{431.1}\, \underline{d}_1 - \underset{(2.50)}{347.0}\, \underline{d}_2 - \underset{(7.09)}{992.1}\, \underline{d}_3 - \underset{(0.04)}{8.8}\, \underline{dumb1} -$$

$$- \underset{(2.85)}{595.0}\, \underline{dumw3} + \underset{(1.20)}{2{,}734.5}$$

Estimation period: 1970:I-1979:IV

$\bar{R}^2 = 0.85$

SR = 255.18

Q(12) = 11.58

h = 0.43

55. Investment in dwellings

$$i_{wo} = \underset{(5.33)}{0.477}\, i_{wo_{-1}} + \underset{(3.05)}{0.040}\left(\tfrac{1}{4}\sum_{j=0}^{3} y_{nnim_{-j}}\right) - \underset{(3.36)}{155.299}\left(\tfrac{1}{2}\sum_{j=0}^{1} r_{l_{-j}}\right) +$$

$$+ \underset{(-)}{2.0}\, \underline{h}_{pb} - \underset{(2.51)}{160.8}\, \underline{d}_1 + \underset{(0.28)}{19.5}\, \underline{d}_2 + \underset{(3.16)}{198.9}\, \underline{d}_3 + \underset{(1.69)}{189.5}\, \underline{dumb1} +$$

$$+ \underset{(5.81)}{1{,}196.4}\, \underline{dumwl} - \underset{(2.34)}{1{,}067.6}$$

Estimation period: 1970:I-1979:IV

$\bar{R}^2 = 0.95$

SR = 140.36

Q(12) = 14.24

h = 1.63

56. Exports of goods

$$\ln b_{-saog} = \underset{(5.67)}{0.715} \ln b_{-saog_{-1}} - \underset{(1.76)}{0.341} \ln (p_{b_{-saog}}/p_{bf}) +$$

$$+ \underset{(10.73)}{0.979} \ln \underline{m}_w - \underset{(4.54)}{0.702} \ln \underline{m}_{w_{-1}} +$$

$$+ (1 - \underset{(3.09)}{0.518}\, B^4)\varepsilon + \underset{(2.33)}{1.568}$$

Estimation period: 1970:I-1979:IV

$\bar{R}^2 = 0.98$

SR = 0.0249

Q(11) = 7.12

57. Imports of goods

$$\ln m_{-saog} = \underset{(-)}{0.6} \ln m_{-saog_{-1}} - \underset{(2.28)}{0.297} \ln (p_{m_{-saog}}/p_v) +$$

$$+ \underset{(6.01)}{0.992} (\ln v - \underset{(-)}{0.6} \ln v_{-1}) + \underset{(5.20)}{0.023} (n - \underset{(-)}{0.6} n_{-1}) +$$

$$+ \underset{(2.79)}{0.415} \ln q_{k_{-1}} - \underset{(2.02)}{0.048} \underline{d}_1 - \underset{(3.93)}{0.068} \underline{d}_2 -$$

$$- \underset{(6.72)}{0.179} \underline{d}_3 - \underset{(2.16)}{0.031} \underline{dumb1} + \underset{(0.80)}{0.992}$$

Estimation period: 1970:I-1979:IV

$\bar{R}^2$ = 0.93

SR = 0.0218

Q(12) = 33.08

h = -2.29

58. Gross output of enterprises

$$y = \underset{(2.44)}{0.157} y_{-1} + \underset{(14.42)}{0.970} v_b - \underset{(2.87)}{0.131} \Sigma n_{-1} + \underset{(0.44)}{241.1} \underline{d}_1 +$$

$$+ \underset{(3.21)}{1{,}049.9} \underline{d}_2 + \underset{(7.51)}{3{,}100.9} \underline{d}_3 - \underset{(1.79)}{838.9} \underline{dumb1} - \underset{(0.57)}{993.4}$$

Estimation period: 1970:I-1979:IV

$\bar{R}^2$ = 0.99

SR = 660.02

Q(12) = 10.09

h = -1.04

Demand for labour

59. $$k_a = 0.015 \left[1 + 0.373 \left(\left(1/4 \sum_{j=0}^{3} (i_b^g - \dot{p}_{y_{bm}})_{-j}\right) - \right.\right.$$

$$\left.\left. - \underline{\mu} - 2.75\ \underline{dumb4} + 2.88\ \underline{dumw2}\right) \frac{1}{\underline{\mu}}\right] k_{-1}$$

60. $k = k_{-1} + i_{-sa} - k_a - \underline{dumb3}$

61. $a^* = 0.0188\ [1 + 0.528\ (1 - \frac{h}{\underline{h}_0})\ ]\ k\ .\ e^{-1.170 \sum_{j=0}^{t} \mu_{-j}/100}$

62. $y^*_{bm} = \frac{1}{\underline{\varkappa}}\ .\ k$

63. $q_k = y_{bm}/y^*_{bm}$

64. $a = a^* - 0.454\ (1 - \frac{1}{4} \sum_{j=0}^{3} q_{k_{-j}})a^* - 25.7\ \underline{d}_1 - 6.9\ \underline{d}_2 +$

$+ 19.0\ \underline{d}_3 + 13.6\ \underline{d}_4 - 53.58\ \underline{dumb5} + 127.82\ \underline{dumw4}$

Estimation period: 1970:I-1979:IV
SR = 14.39
$\hat{\varrho}$ = 0.60

65. Supply of labour

$$a_a = \underset{(13.06)}{0.412}\ \underline{a}_p - \underset{(2.33)}{0.314}\ (\tfrac{1}{4} \sum_{j=1}^{4} U_{-j}) + \underset{(4.02)}{50.39}\ \underline{dnpj} +$$

$$+ \underset{(3.36)}{9.67}\ \underline{d}_1 - \underset{(2.51)}{9.12}\ \underline{d}_2 + \underset{(0.50)}{1.38}\ \underline{d}_3 - \underset{(1.42)}{8.94}\ \underline{dumb1} +$$

$$+ \underset{(1.52)}{637.6} + (1/(1 + \underset{(3.36)}{0.588}\ B - \underset{(2.11)}{0.353}\ B^2))\varepsilon$$

Estimation period: 1970:I-1979:IV
$\overline{R}^2$ = 0.99
SR = 6.77
Q(10)= 10.75

66. Wage determination, enterprises

$$\ln l^g_b = \underset{(-)}{0.925}\ \ln p_{cg} + \underset{(41.91)}{0.860}\ \ln a_g + \underset{(8.45)}{0.457}\ \ln ((TL + PL)/L) -$$

$$- \underset{(1.36)}{0.713}\ (\tfrac{1}{2} \sum_{j=0}^{1} \Delta \frac{U}{a}_{-j}) + \underset{(2.85)}{0.024}\ \underline{dum70} - \underset{(3.03)}{0.031}\ \underline{dumw2} +$$

$$+\,0.016\ \underline{dum75/76} - 6.535$$
$$(2.86) \qquad\qquad (48.85)$$

Estimation period: 1970:I-1979:IV

$\bar{R}^2 = 0.99$
SR $= 0.00974$
Q(12) $= 8.85$
DW $= 1.71$

67. $$p_{cg} = p_{cg_{-1}} (1 + \alpha\, (p_{c_{-1}} - p_{c_{-3}})/p_{c_{-3}})$$

68. $$a_g = a_{g_{-1}} (1 + 1/4 \sum_{j=0}^{3} ((\frac{y_{bm}}{a} - \frac{y_{bm_{-4}}}{a_{-4}}) / \frac{y_{bm_{-4}}}{a_{-4}})_{-j} \cdot \beta)$$

69. Wage determination, government

$$\dot{i}_{ov} = 0.874\ \dot{i}_b^g + 1.954\ \underline{d}_1 - 1.895\ \underline{d}_2 - 0.445\ \underline{d}_3 -$$
$$(6.79) \qquad (2.47) \qquad (3.76) \qquad (0.67)$$

$$-\ 3.355\ \underline{dumb2} + 1.663\ \underline{dumw3} + 0.205$$
$$(3.23) \qquad (1.76) \qquad (0.56)$$

Estimation period: 1970:I-1979:IV

$\bar{R}^2 = 0.85$
SR $= 1.03$
Q(11) $= 16.48$
$\hat{\varrho} = -0.34$

70. Price of private consumption

$$\dot{p}_c = 0.471\ (1/2 \sum_{j=0}^{1} \dot{i}^g_{b_{-j}}) - 0.115\ (\dot{y}_{bm} - \dot{a}) +$$
$$(4.25) \qquad\qquad (2.68)$$

$$+\,0.20\ \dot{p}_{mc} - 1.817\ \underline{d}_1 + 0.632\ \underline{d}_2 - 1.768\ \underline{d}_3 -$$
$$(-) \qquad (3.68) \qquad (1.80) \qquad (5.79)$$

$$-\ 2.036\ \underline{dumb2} + 1.207$$
$$(2.88) \qquad (3.98)$$

Estimation period: 1970:I-1979:IV

$\bar{R}^2 = 0.73$

SR = 0.63

Q(12) = 14.18

DW = 1.68

An alternative is:

$$\dot{p}_c = \underset{(10.71)}{0.779} \left(\tfrac{1}{2} \sum_{j=0}^{1} i^g_{b_{-j}}\right) - \underset{(2.87)}{0.141} (\dot{y}_{bm} - \dot{a}) + \underset{(-)}{0.221} \dot{p}_{mc} -$$

$$- \underset{(4.33)}{2.289} \underline{d}_1 + \underset{(0.58)}{0.220} \underline{d}_2 - \underset{(5.91)}{2.169} \underline{d}_3 - \underset{(2.64)}{2.132} \underline{dumb2} + \underset{(2.20)}{0.635}$$

Estimation period: 1970:I-1979:IV

$\bar{R}^2 = 0.94$

SR = 0.71

Q(12) = 17.44

h = 1.49

71. Price of other gross fixed investment

$$\dot{p}_{i_{-sa}} = \underset{(3.68)}{0.392} \left(\tfrac{1}{2} \sum_{j=0}^{1} i^g_{b_{-j}}\right) - \underset{(3.39)}{0.141} (\dot{y}_{bm} - \dot{a}) +$$

$$+ \underset{(2.85)}{0.423} \left(\tfrac{1}{4} \sum_{j=0}^{3} \dot{p}_{mi_{-j}}\right) + \underset{(1.49)}{0.052} \dot{p}_k +$$

$$+ \underset{(1.13)}{0.217} \left(\tfrac{1}{4} \sum_{j=0}^{3} \dot{q}_{k_{-j}}\right) - \underset{(3.79)}{4.171} \underline{dum73/1} - \underset{(0.86)}{0.947} \underline{dumb2}$$

Estimation period: 1970:I-1979:IV

$\bar{R}^2 = 0.81$

SR = 0.97

Q(11) = 10.25

$\hat{\varrho} = -0.36$

72. Price of exports of goods

$$\dot{p}_{b_{-saog}} = \underset{(1.51)}{0.220}\, i^{g}_{b_{-1}} - \underset{(5.21)}{0.307}\, (\dot{y}_{bm} - \dot{a}) +$$

$$+ \underset{(1.20)}{0.168}\, (½ \sum_{j=0}^{1} \dot{p}_{mgh_{-j}}) + \underset{(2.50)}{0.125}\, \dot{p}_{k_{-1}} + \underset{(3.52)}{0.491}\, \dot{p}_{bf} +$$

$$+ \underset{(1.86)}{0.514}\, (¼ \sum_{j=0}^{3} \dot{q}_{k_{-j}}) - \underset{(3.66)}{3.939}\, \underline{dumw3} - \underset{(0.87)}{0.382}$$

Estimation period: 1970:I-1979:IV
$\bar{R}^2$ = 0.72
SR = 1.24
Q(12) = 9.11
DW = 2.36

73. Price of autonomous expenditure

$$\dot{p}_{x} = \underset{(4.85)}{0.513}\, \dot{p}_{c} + \underset{(-)}{0.188}\, \dot{p}_{m_{-saog}} + \underset{(2.94)}{0.299}\, \dot{p}_{i_{-sa}} -$$

$$- \underset{(1.39)}{0.613}\, \underline{d}_1 - \underset{(2.43)}{0.917}\, \underline{d}_2 - \underset{(0.93)}{0.406}\, \underline{d}_3 + \underset{(3.16)}{0.987}$$

Estimation period: 1970:I-1979:IV
$\bar{R}^2$ = 0.82
SR = 0.83
Q(12) = 10.75
DW = 2.34

74. Price of investment in dwellings

$$\dot{p}_{i_{wo}} = \underset{(3.29)}{0.401}\, \dot{p}_{i} + \underset{(-)}{0.599}\, \dot{p}_{c} + \underset{(1.17)}{0.473}\, \underline{d}_1 - \underset{(1.36)}{0.505}\, \underline{d}_2 +$$

$$+ \underset{(1.37)}{0.563}\, \underline{d}_3 + \underset{(1.60)}{0.436}$$

Estimation period: 1970:I-1979:IV
$\bar{R}^2$ = 0.49
SR = 0.83
Q(12) = 18.72
DW = 2.00

75. Price of stockbuilding

$$\dot{p}_n = \underset{(-)}{0.288}\ \dot{p}_c + \underset{(6.06)}{0.712}\ \dot{p}_m + \underset{(10.26)}{24.120}\ \underline{dum79} - \underset{(0.21)}{0.143}$$

Estimation period: 1970:I-1979:IV
$\bar{R}^2$ = 0.83
SR = 2.51
Q(11) = 17.33
$\hat{\varrho}$ = 0.40

76. Number of unemployed persons under the Unemployment Act

$$WW = \underset{(3.59)}{0.146}\ U + \underset{(4.91)}{0.278}\ \Delta_4 U + \underset{(14.16)}{20.991}\ \underline{d}_1 + \underset{(1.80)}{2.541}\ \underline{d}_2 -$$

$$- \underset{(7.30)}{8.794}\ \underline{d}_3 + \underset{(3.14)}{22.380}$$

Estimation period: 1970:I-1979:IV
$\bar{R}^2$ = 0.96
SR = 3.78
Q(11) = 6.51
$\hat{\varrho}$ = 0.77

Technical and definitional equations

Output

77. $Y_{bnpm} = Y_{bm} + Y_{ov} + (\underline{B}_p - \underline{M}_p)$

78. $y_{bnpm} = y_{bm} + y_{ov} + (\underline{b}_p - \underline{m}_p)$

79. $Y_{bm} = V + \underline{I}_{sa} + B_{saog} + N - M_{-saog} - M_{saog} - M_s -$

$- \underline{F}_o - \underline{TK}_{ov} - \underline{LI}_{ov}$

80. $v_b = v - (\underline{f}_o + tk_{ov} + li_{ov} - \underline{i}_{sa} - \underline{b}_{saog})$

81. $n = y - v_b$

82. $y_{bm} = y - m_{-saog} - \underline{m}_{saog} - \underline{m}_s$

83. $\Sigma n = \Sigma n_{-1} + n$

84. $Y_{ov} = L_{ov} + \underline{F}_o + \underline{TK}_{ov}$

85. $y_{ov} = l_{ov} + \underline{f}_o + tk_{ov}$

86. $Y_{nnpm} = Y_{bnpm} - \underline{F}_b - \underline{F}_o$

87. $y_{nnpm} = y_{bnpm} - \underline{f}_b - \underline{f}_o$

88. $y_{nnim} = y_{nnpm} + R_p$

89. $R_p = (B/p_{m_{-p}} - B/p_{b_{-p}}) \,.\, 100 + \underline{R}_{p_{rest}}$

Expenditure

90. $V = C + I_{-sa} + I_{wo} + \underline{X} + B_{-saog} + \underline{B}_s$

91. $v = c + i_{-sa} + i_{wo} + x + b_{-saog} + \underline{b}_s$

92. $I = I_{-sa} + \underline{I}_{sa} + I_{wo}$

93. $i = i_{-sa} + \underline{i}_{sa} + i_{wo}$

94. $X' = \underline{X} + L_{ov} - \underline{LI}_{ov}$

of which external transactions

95. $B = B_{-saog} + B_{saog} + \underline{B}_s + \underline{B}_p$

96. $b = b_{-saog} + \underline{b}_{saog} + \underline{b}_s + \underline{b}_p$

97. $M = M_{-saog} + M_{saog} + M_s + \underline{M}_p$

98. $m = m_{-saog} + \underline{m}_{saog} + \underline{m}_s + \underline{m}_p$

99. $E = (B - M) + \underline{D}_s$

Factor income

100. $Y_{nnpf} = L + Z + (\underline{B}_p - \underline{M}_p)$

101. $L = L_b + L_{ov}$

102. $l_b = l_b^g \cdot \gamma$

103. $L_b = a_l \cdot l_b$

104. $L_{ov} = \underline{a}_{ov} \cdot l_{ov}$

105. $Z = Y_{bm} - L_b - \underline{F}_b - TK_{-s} + \underline{TK}_{ov}$

106. $Z_o = Z - TLZ$

107. $TLZ = \underline{a}_z \cdot l_b$

108. $Y_{nf} = L_b + Z$

109. $A_q = ((a_l + \underline{a}_z)/a_l)\ L_b/Y_{nf}$

110. $A_q^g = A_q - \underline{A}_q^{cor}$

Redistribution of income

111. $Y_{nbm} = Y_{nbf} + TK_{-s}$

112. $Y_{nbf} = L_d + O_d + Z_d + P + T - Ui - TR$

Taxes

113. $TL = \pi_l \cdot L$

114. $TO = \pi_o . O$

115. $TZ = \pi_z . Z$

116. $TK_{-s} = \pi_{k_{-s}} (C + I + \underline{X} + B_{-saog} + B_{saog} + \underline{B}_s)$

117. $T = TL + TO + TZ$

Payments and transfers, contributions and premiums

118. $Ui_{ww} = 0.80\ \psi\ .\ \iota^g_b\ .\ WW$

119. $Ui_{slp} = \omega\ .\ \iota^g_b$

120. $Ui = Ui_{ww} + Ui_{slp}$

121. $Ui_{wr} = \phi\ .\ \iota^g_b (U - WW)$

122. $TR_{-wr} = \chi\ .\ \iota^g_b$

123. $TR = TR_{-wr} + Ui_{wr}$

124. $O = Ui + TR$

125. $P = Ui - \underline{P}_g + \underline{P}_{aut}$

126. $PL = \lambda_l . P$

127. $PO = \lambda_o . P$

128. $PZ = (1 - \lambda_l - \lambda_o) P$

Disposable incomes

129. $Z_{od} = Z_o - (TZ - (TL/L)\ TLZ)$

130. $TLZ_d = (1 - TL/L)\ TLZ - PZ$

131. $Z_d = Z_{od} + TLZ_d$

132. $L_d = L - TL - PL$

133. $L_{dz} = L_d + TLZ_d$

134. $O_d = O - TO - PO$

135. $W_d = L_{dz} + O_d$

Budget equation of the government

136. $FT_o^{tr} = X' + TR + \underline{LI}_{ov} + \underline{P}_g + Re + \underline{TR}_k - T - TK_{-s} - \underline{NT}$

Other equations

137. $U = a_a - a_l - \underline{a}_z - \underline{a}_{ov}$

138. $a_l = a - \underline{a}_z$

139. $li_{ov} = \underline{LI}_{ov} \cdot \underline{lc}_{ov}/(L_{ov} - \underline{LI}_{ov})$

140. $l_{ov} = li_{ov} + \underline{lc}_{ov}$

141. $tk_{ov} = \underline{TK}_{ov} \cdot c/C$

142. $p_k = 0.01\,(r_l + 1.4)\,p_{i_{-sa}} \cdot 10.531$

C. The equations to link the monetary and real economic blocks

Exchange rates and balance-of-payments items

143. $p_{bf} = \underline{p}_{bf} \cdot e_{\$}^{0.103} \cdot e_{DM}^{0.219}$

144. $p_{mc} = \underline{p}_{mc} \cdot e_{\$}^{0.085} \cdot e_{DM}^{0.377}$

145. $p_{mi} = \underline{p}_{mi} \cdot e_{\$}^{0.085} \cdot e_{DM}^{0.377}$

146. $p_{mgh} = \underline{p}_{mgh} \cdot e_{\$}^{0.250} \cdot e_{DM}^{0.110}$

147. $p_{m_s} = \underline{p}_{m_s} \cdot e_{\$}^{0.317} \cdot e_{DM}^{0.144}$

148. $p_{m_{-sa}} = \underline{p}_{m_{-sa}} \cdot e_{\$}^{0.340} \cdot e_{DM}^{0.240}$

149. $p_{b_{og}} = \underline{p}_{b_{og}} \cdot e_{\$}^{1.0}$

150. $p_{m_{og}} = \underline{p}_{m_{og}} \cdot e_{\$}^{1.0}$

151. $B_{saog} = \underline{B}_{sa} + B_{og}$

152. $M_{saog} = \underline{M}_{sa} + M_{og}$

153. $B_{-sa} = B - \underline{B}_{sa} - \underline{B}_{p}$

154. $m_{-sa} = m_{-saog} + \underline{m}_{saog} + \underline{m}_{s} - \underline{m}_{sa}$

155. $M_{-saog} = M_{-sa} - M_{og} - M_{s}$

Interest charges on government debt

156. $Re = \bar{r}\,(VAS + VLS)$

157. $\bar{r} = \underset{(8.01)}{0.782} \left(\sum_{j=4}^{64} \pi_{-j} \cdot r_{l_{-j}} \right) + \underset{(-)}{0.100} \left(1/20 \sum_{j=0}^{19} r_{sc_{-j}} \right) + \underset{(3.71)}{0.097}\, r_k +$

$$+ 0.388 \underline{d}_1 - 1.777 \underline{d}_2 - 0.419 \underline{d}_3 + 0.797$$
$$(1.89) \quad (8.68) \quad (2.13) \quad (1.13)$$

Estimation period: 1970:II-1979:IV
$\bar{R}^2 = 0.87$
SR = 0.44
Q(12) = 14.44
DW = 1.22

Government's financial deficit

158. $FT_o = FT_o^{tr} + \underline{VFT}_o$

Liquidity ratio

159. $LQ = M2 / \sum_{j=0}^{3} Y_{nnpm_{-j}}$

Expenditure

160. $MW = \frac{1}{4} \sum_{j=0}^{3} (\underline{m}_w \cdot p_{bf})_{-j}$

161. $IB = I + N$

Output and incomes

162. $Y_{nnpmb} = Y_{nnpm} + \underline{D}_s$

163. $SA = Y_{bm} + M_{-saog} + M_{saog}$

164. $sa = y_{bm} + m_{-saog} + \underline{m}_{saog}$

Appendix II. Explanation of symbols used

In the list of symbols given below, the underlined variables are exogenous. For the endogenous variables, the equations explaining them are given in parentheses. For a number of endogenous value, volume and price variables from the real economic sector, no equation numbers are listed, as Appendix I does not include the identities for converting volume into value variables or conversely.

a	(64)	Employment in enterprises, man-years
a^*	(61)	Full capacity employment in enterprises, man-years
a_a	(65)	Supply of labour (labour force), man-years
a_g	(68)	Labour productivity, on an annual basis
a_l	(138)	Employment of wage earners in enterprises, man-years
$\underline{a}_{ov}$		Employment of public servants, man-years
$\underline{a}_p$		Working-age population (persons aged 14-65)
A_q	(109)	Labour income ratio in enterprises
$\underline{A}_q^{cor}$		Adjustment to labour income ratio for income from natural gas and oil exploitation and quarrying, housing and public utilities
A_q^g	(110)	Labour income ratio, adjusted for income from natural gas and oil exploitation and quarrying, housing and public utilities
$\underline{a}_z$		Number of the self-employed, man-years
B	(95)	Total exports, current prices
b	(96)	Ditto, 1977 prices

B_{og}		Exports of oil and gas, current prices
$\underline{b}_{og}$		Ditto, 1977 prices
$\underline{B}_{p}$		Factor income received from the rest of the world
$\underline{b}_{p}$		Ditto, 1977 prices
$\underline{B}_{s}$		Exports of services, current prices
$\underline{b}_{s}$		Ditto, 1977 prices
$\underline{B}_{sa}$		Exports of ships and aircraft, current prices
$\underline{b}_{sa}$		Ditto, 1977 prices
B_{-sa}	(153)	Exports of goods and services, excluding ships and aircraft, current prices
b_{-sa}		Ditto, 1977 prices
B_{-saog}		Exports of goods, excluding ships, aircraft, oil and gas, current prices
b_{-saog}	(56)	Ditto, 1977 prices
B_{saog}	(151)	Exports of ships, aircraft, oil and gas, current prices
$\underline{b}_{saog}$		Ditto, 1977 prices
BBIN	(21)	Foreign holdings of domestic liabilities
BL	(10)	Short-term bank lending to the private sector
BNIB	(5)	Private sector holdings of foreign liabilities
BTB	(17)	Balance sheet total of the banks
$BTB \mid S_{fs}$	(14)	Balance sheet total of the institutional investors, excluding savings deposits with these institutions

BTOT	(18)	Balance sheet total of the banks and institutional investors
C		Private consumption, current prices
c	(53)	Ditto, 1977 prices
cadm	(40)	Spot exchange rate of Deutsche mark against parity
CH	(6)	Currency
CH_{cb}	(41)	Currency issued by the central bank (bank notes in circulation)
$\underline{CH}_{ro}$		Currency issued by the central government
D	(7)	Demand deposits
$\underline{d}_1, \underline{d}_2, \underline{d}_3, \underline{d}_4$		Seasonal dummy variables
$\underline{d}_1$ 70/74, $\underline{d}_2$ 70/74, $\underline{d}_3$ 70/74, $\underline{d}_4$ 70/74		Seasonal dummy variables 1970:I-1974:IV
$\underline{D}_s$		Net income transfers to the rest of the world
$\underline{DA}_b$		Miscellaneous bank assets
dnpj		Youth participation rate on the labour market
dum70		Dummy variable for the Fl. 400 wage increase in 1970
dum73/1		Dummy variable in investment price equation
dum75/76		Dummy variable for wage measures 1975-1976
dum79		Dummy variable for oil price rise 1979
dumb1,b2, b3,b4,b5, b6		Dummy variables for 1977 break in series in the National Accounts and for the change in the definition of savings (b6)

$\underline{dumw1, w2,}$ $\underline{w3, w4}$		Dummy variables for harsh 1979 winter
$\underline{dum1975HKO}$		Dummy variable in equation for trade credit received
$\underline{dum1973r}_{bl}$		Dummy variable for extraordinary money market conditions in 1973:IV
$\underline{dumkwart2}$		Dummy variable in connection with banks' net foreign assets
$\underline{dump}$		Dummy variable in exchange rate equation
$dumr_{bl}$	(33)	Dummy variable for extra surcharge on banks' overdraft rates
$\underline{dumr}_{k}$		Dummy variable for periods marked by use of interest rate in support of the guilder
$\underline{dumr}_{k}2$		Dummy variable for 1976:III and IV in connection with foreign exchange market conditions
DVL'	(52)	Tension variable for (net) capital market borrowing
E	(99)	Balance on current account, on a transactions basis
$e_{\$}$	(36)	Exchange rate of the dollar against the guilder
$\hat{e}_{\$}$	(38)	Expected change in the exchange rate of the dollar against the guilder
e_{DM}	(39)	Exchange rate of the Deutsche mark against the guilder
$\underline{\bar{e}}_{DM}$		Ditto, parity
$\underline{e}_{DM.\$}$		Exchange rate of the dollar against the Deutsche mark
$\underline{F}_{b}$		Depreciation, enterprises, current prices
$\underline{f}_{b}$		Ditto, 1977 prices
$\underline{F}_{o}$		Depreciation, government, current prices

$\underline{f}_o$		Ditto, 1977 prices
FA	(1)	Financial assets of the private sector
FT_o	(158)	Financial deficit of the government, on a cash basis
FT_o^*	(42)	Financial deficit of the government, on a cash basis, including miscellaneous items
FT_o^{tr}	(136)	Financial deficit of the government, on a transactions basis
GLR	(16)	Banks' borrowed reserves
$\underline{h}$		Number of hours worked in enterprises
$\underline{h}_0$		Number of hours worked in enterprises in 1970:I
$\underline{h}_{pb}$		Number of effective hours worked in construction industry, index
ΔHK_{bu}	(26)	Net external trade credit
ΔHKO_{bu}	(24)	External trade credit received
ΔHKV_{bu}	(25)	External trade credit granted
I	(92)	Gross fixed investment of enterprises, current prices
i	(93)	Ditto, 1977 prices
$\underline{I}_{sa}$		Gross investment of enterprises in ships and aircraft, current prices
$\underline{i}_{sa}$		Ditto, 1977 prices
I_{-sa}		Other gross fixed investment of enterprises, excluding ships and aircraft, current prices
i_{-sa}	(54)	Ditto, 1977 prices

I_{wo}		Gross investment in dwellings, enterprises, current prices
i_{wo}	(55)	Ditto, 1977 prices
IB	(161)	Gross investment of enterprises, including stockbuilding, current prices
IR	(47)	Gold and foreign exchange holdings (stock of international reserves)
$\underline{IR}_{aut}$		Ditto, autonomous part
k	(60)	Stock of capital goods, 1977 prices
k_a	(59)	Scrappage of capital goods, 1977 prices
KOS_b	(46)	Short-term government debt held by the banks
$\underline{KOS}_{cb}$		Short-term govenment debt held by the central bank
KOS_{ps}	(9)	Short-term government debt held by the private sector
$\underline{kr}$		Dummy variable for periods of credit restriction
$\underline{KT}_{ro}$		Central government's cash and deposits
L	(101)	Total wage and salary bill
L_b	(103)	Wage and salary bill in enterprises
l_b	(102)	Wage and salary bill per worker in enterprises
l_b^g	(66)	Ditto, adjusted for absence due to sickness
L_d	(132)	Disposable income of wage earners, excluding the self-employed
L_{dz}	(133)	Ditto, including the self-employed
L_{ov}	(104)	Government wage and salary bill

l_{ov}	(140)	Ditto, 1977 prices
l_{ov}	(69)	Wage and salary bill per public servant
$\underline{LB}_{lo}$		Liquid assets held by the local government
$\underline{lc}_{ov}$		Government wages and salaries (consumptive expenditure), 1977 prices
$\underline{LI}_{ov}$		Government wage and salary bill for investment under own management
li_{ov}	(139)	Ditto, 1977 prices
LK_b	(50)	Capital market investment of the banks
$\underline{LK}_{b,o}$		Capital market investment of the banks with the government
$LK_{b,ps}$	(12)	Capital market investment of the banks with the private sector
$\underline{LK}_{cb,o}$		Long-term funds raised from the central bank by the government
$LK_{fs,gb}$	(13)	Capital market investment of the institutional investors with households and enterprises
LK_{gb}	(15)	Capital market investment of households and enterprises
LK_{ps}	(4)	Capital market investment of the private sector
$LK_{ps,b}$	(48)	Long-term funds raised from the private sector by the banks
$LK_{ps,o}$	(49)	Long-term lending by the private sector to the government
LOG_{ps}	(11)	Long-term funds raised by the private sector
LQ	(159)	Liquidity ratio

LR	(27)	Balance on current account, on a cash basis
$\underline{LRRV}$		Statistical discrepancies between current account on a cash and on a transactions basis
M	(97)	Total imports, current prices
m	(98)	Ditto, 1977 prices
M_{og}		Imports of oil and gas, current prices
$\underline{m}_{og}$		Ditto, 1977 prices
$\underline{M}_{p}$		Factor income paid to the rest of the world
$\underline{m}_{p}$		Ditto, 1977 prices
M_{s}		Imports of services, current prices
$\underline{m}_{s}$		Ditto, 1977 prices
$\underline{M}_{sa}$		Imports of ships and aircraft, current prices
$\underline{m}_{sa}$		Ditto, 1977 prices
M_{-sa}		Imports of goods and services, excluding ships and aircraft, current prices
m_{-sa}	(154)	Ditto, 1977 prices
M_{-saog}	(155)	Imports of goods, excluding ships, aircraft, oil and gas, current prices
m_{-saog}	(57)	Ditto, 1977 prices
M_{saog}	(152)	Imports of ships, aircraft, oil and gas, current prices
$\underline{m}_{saog}$		Ditto, 1977 prices
$\underline{m}_{w}$		Volume of reweighted world imports, 1977 prices

MW	(160)	Reweighted world imports
M2	(2)	Domestic money stock
N		Increase in stocks and work in progress (stockbuilding), current prices
n	(81)	Ditto, 1977 prices
Σn	(83)	Stocks and work in progress, 1977 prices
NBA_b	(23)	Net foreign assets of the banks
ΔNBA_{cb}	(37)	Foreign exchange market interventions by the central bank
$\underline{NBA}_o$		Net foreign assets of the government
NBA_{ps}	(22)	Net foreign assets of the private sector
$\underline{NBARV}$		Statistical discrepancies with regard to net foreign assets of the banks
$\underline{NT}$		Non-tax revenues of the government
O	(124)	Transfer income
O_d	(134)	Disposable transfer income
P	(125)	Total of social insurance contributions and pension and life assurance premiums
$\underline{P}_{aut}$		Net other income and expenditure of social insurance funds, pension funds and life assurance companies
p_b		Price index of total exports (1977=100)
$p_{b_{og}}$	(149)	Price index of exports of oil and gas (1977=100)
$\underline{p}_{b_{og}}$		Ditto, in dollars

$p_{b_{-saog}}$	(72)	Price index of exports of goods, excluding ships, aircraft, oil and gas (1977=100)
$p_{b_{-p}}$		Price index of total exports, excluding factor income received from the rest of the world (1977=100)
p_{bf}	(143)	Price index of goods exports of competitor countries, reweighted (1977=100)
$\underline{p}_{bf}$		Ditto, in foreign currencies
p_c	(70)	Price index of private consumption (1977=100)
p_{cg}	(67)	Wage compensation for price increases
$\underline{p}_{DU}$		Price index of the Federal Republic of Germany's exports, in Deutsche marks
$\underline{p}_g$		Transfers of the central government to social insurance funds
p_i		Price index of gross fixed investment of enterprises (1977=100)
$p_{i_{-sa}}$	(71)	Price index of other gross fixed investment of enterprises, excluding ships and aircraft (1977=100)
$p_{i_{wo}}$	(74)	Price index of investment in dwellings (1977=100)
p_k	(142)	Price index of capital (1977=100)
p_m		Price index of total imports (1977=100)
$p_{m_{og}}$	(150)	Price index of imports of oil and gas (1977=100)
$\underline{p}_{m_{og}}$		Ditto, in dollars
p_{m_s}	(147)	Price index of imports of services (1977=100)
$\underline{p}_{m_s}$		Ditto, in foreign currencies

$p_{m_{-sa}}$	(148)	Price index of imports of goods and services, excluding ships and aircraft (1977=100)
$\underline{p}_{m_{-sa}}$		Ditto, in foreign currencies
$p_{m_{-saog}}$		Price index of imports of goods, excluding ships, aircraft, oil and gas (1977=100)
$p_{m_{-p}}$		Price index of total imports, excluding factor income paid to the rest of the world (1977=100)
p_{mc}	(144)	Price index of imports of consumer goods (1977=100)
$\underline{p}_{mc}$		Ditto, in foreign currencies
p_{mgh}	(146)	Price index of imports of raw materials and intermediate goods (1977=100)
$\underline{p}_{mgh}$		Ditto, in foreign currencies
p_{mi}	(145)	Price index of imports of capital goods (1977=100)
$\underline{p}_{mi}$		Ditto, in foreign currencies
p_n	(75)	Price index of increase in stocks and work in progress (1977=100)
p_{sa}		Price index of total sales (1977=100)
p_v		Price index of total expenditure, excluding stockbuilding, government wage and salary bill, investment in and exports of ships and aircraft, and factor income received from the rest of the world (1977=100)
$\underline{p}_{VS}$		Price index of United States exports, in dollars
$\underline{p}_w$		Price index of dwellings (1977=100)
p_x	(73)	Price index of autonomous expenditure (1977=100)

$p_{y_{bm}}$		Price index of gross value added in enterprises, market prices (1977=100)
$p_{y_{bnpm}}$		Price index of gross national product, market prices (1977=100)
PL	(126)	Social insurance contributions paid in respect of wage and salary bill, including pension and life assurance premiums
PO	(127)	Social insurance contributions paid by recipients of transfer incomes
PZ	(128)	Social insurance contributions paid by the self-employed
q_k	(63)	Utilization rate of capital
$\bar{r}$	(157)	Average interest rate on government debt
r_{bl}	(33)	Interest rate on short-term bank loans
$\underline{r}_{bl}^{bu}$		Average discount rate in the Federal Republic of Germany, the United Kingdom and the United States
$\underline{r}_{cb}$		Discount rate on promissory notes
r_d	(30)	Interest rate on ordinary current-account balances
r_k	(28)	Short-term interest rate
$\underline{r}_k^{DU}$		Short-term interest rate in the Federal Republic of Germany (interest rate on Euro-Deutsche mark deposits)
$\underline{r}_k^{VS}$		Short-term interest rate in the United States (interest rate on Euro-dollar deposits)
r_l	(29)	Long-term interest rate (average of latest three long-term central government bonds)
$\underline{r}_l^{bu}$		Foreign long-term interest rate

$\underline{r}_l^{DU}$		Long-term interest rate in the Federal Republic of Germany
$\underline{r}_l^{VS}$		Long-term interest rate in the United States
r_{M2}	(35)	Interest rate on domestic money stock
R_p	(89)	Improvement in terms of trade on 1977
$\underline{R}_{p_{rest}}$		Ditto, adjustment for statistical discrepancies
r_s	(31)	Interest rate on savings deposits
r_{sc}	(32)	Interest rate on three-month Treasury paper
r_{TV}	(34)	Interest rate on time deposits and foreign-currency deposits
$\underline{RBO}$		Items in transit, including other exogenous items on the balance of payments on a cash basis
Re	(156)	Interest payments on government debt
S	(3)	Savings deposits of the private sector
S_b	(19)	Savings deposits with banks
S_{fs}	(20)	Savings deposits with institutional investors
SA	(163)	Total sales
sa	(164)	Ditto, 1977 prices
SSCH	(45)	Treasury's balance at the central bank
$\underline{SWAP}$		Dollar swaps between the central bank and the authorized banks
T	(117)	Direct taxes on wage, transfer and other income
$\underline{TK}_{ov}$		Indirect taxes paid by the government to itself

tk_{ov}	(141)	Ditto, 1977 prices
TK_{-s}	(116)	Indirect taxes less balances of price-reducing subsidies and price-increasing levies
TL	(113)	Direct taxes on wage income
TLZ	(107)	Imputed wage income of the self-employed
TLZ_d	(130)	Imputed disposable wage income of the self-employed
TO	(114)	Direct taxes on transfer income
TR	(123)	Government transfers to households (net)
$\underline{tr}$		Trend term
$\underline{TR}_k$		Government capital transfers (net)
TR_{-wr}	(122)	Government transfers to households, excluding payments under the Unemployment Provisions Act and the Government Scheme for Unemployed Employees
TV	(8)	Time deposits and foreign-currency deposits (including liquid savings deposits)
TZ	(115)	Direct taxes on other income
U	(137)	Unemployment, man-years
Ui	(120)	Total social insurance benefits and pension and life assurance payments
Ui_{slp}	(119)	Ditto, excluding benefits under the Unemployment Act
Ui_{wr}	(121)	Payments under the Unemployment Provisions Act and the Government Scheme for Unemployed Employees
Ui_{ww}	(118)	Benefits under the Unemployment Act

V	(90)	Total expenditure, excluding stockbuilding, government wage and salary bill, investment in and exports of ships and aircraft, and factor incomes received from the rest of the world, current prices
v	(91)	Ditto, 1977 prices
v_b	(80)	Sales of enterprises, excluding intermediate deliveries, 1977 prices
$\underline{V}_b$		Banks' net wealth
$\underline{V}_{cb}$		Central bank's net wealth
V_{ps}	(51)	Private sector's net wealth
$\underline{V}_w$		Housing stock
VAS	(43)	Long-term government debt
$\underline{VFT}_o$		Difference between government's financial deficit on a cash basis and that on a transactions basis, and statistical discrepancies
VLS	(44)	Short-term government debt
$\underline{VR}$		Banks' balances
W_d	(135)	Disposable wage and transfer income, including that of the self-employed
WW	(76)	Number of (fully) unemployed persons under the Unemployment Act
$\underline{X}$		Autonomous expenditure in current prices (consumptive expenditure of government, excluding government wage and salary bill, and gross fixed investment of government)
x		Ditto, 1977 prices

X'	(94)	Ditto, including wage and salary bill of government
y	(58)	Gross output of enterprises, 1977 market prices
y^*_{bm}	(62)	Production capacity of enterprises, 1977 prices
Y_{bm}	(79)	Gross value added in enterprises, market prices
y_{bm}	(82)	Ditto, 1977 prices
Y_{bnpm}	(77)	Gross national product, market prices
y_{bnpm}	(78)	Ditto, 1977 prices
Y_{nbf}	(112)	Net domestic product, at factor cost
Y_{nbm}	(111)	Ditto, market prices
Y_{nf}	(108)	Net value added in enterprises, at factor cost
y_{nnim}	(88)	Net national income, 1977 market prices
Y_{nnpf}	(100)	Net national product, at factor cost
Y_{nnpm}	(86)	Net national product, market prices
y_{nnpm}	(87)	Ditto, 1977 prices
Y_{nnpmb}	(162)	Net disposable national income
Y_{ov}	(84)	Gross value added by the government, market prices
y_{ov}	(85)	Ditto, 1977 prices
Z	(105)	Other income
Z_d	(131)	Disposable other income
Z_o	(106)	Other income, excluding imputed wage income of the self-employed

Z_{od}	(129)	Disposable other income, excluding imputed disposable wage income of the self-employed
α		Vector with values 0.75, 0.25, 0.75 and 0.25 in the respective quarters of each year (in connection with the scattered effective dates of wage compensation for price increases and of collective labour agreements)
β		Vector with values 0.75, 0.25, and 0 and 0 in the respective quarters of each year (in connection with the scattered effective dates of collective labour agreements)
γ		Adjustment for absence due to sickness
δ_1		Ratio of increase in government's long-term debt to government's financial deficit
δ_2		Ratio of increase in government's short-term debt to government's financial deficit
$\varkappa$		Capital output ratio
λ_l		Share of contributions paid in respect of wage income in total contributions paid
λ_o		Share of contributions paid in respect of transfer income in total contributions paid
μ		Technical progress
π		Survival fractions of government's debt
$\pi_{k_{-s}}$		Burden of indirect taxes
π_l		Burden of direct taxes in respect of wage income
π_o		Burden of direct taxes in respect of transfer income
π_z		Burden of direct taxes in respect of other income

ϕ	Ratio of payment percentages to wages for payments under the Unemployment Provisions Act and the Government Scheme for Unemployed Employees
χ	Ratio of wages to government transfers to households
ψ	Ratio of benefits percentages to wages for benefits under the Unemployment Act
ω	Ratio of wages to social insurance benefits and pension life assurance payments, excluding benefits under the Unemployment Act

Bibliography

Allen, R.G.D., 1968, *Macro-economic Theory, a Mathematical Treatment,* Mac Millan, London/Melbourne/Toronto.

Barro, R.J., 1976, 'Rational expectations and the role of monetary policy', *Journal of Monetary Economics, 2,* pp. 1-32.

Barro, R.J., 1978, 'Unanticipated money, output, and the price level in the United States', *Journal of Political Economy, 86,* pp. 549-580.

Beld, C.A. van den, 1968, 'An experimental medium-term macro model for the Dutch economy', in: M.G. Kendall, ed. *Mathematical Model Building in Economics and Industry,* Griffin, London, pp. 31-48.

Blades, D., 1983, 'Service lives of fixed assets', *OECD Economics and Statistics Department, Working Paper* no. 4.

Bomhoff, E.J., 1982, 'De kunst van het bezuinigen', *Rotterdamse Monetaire Studies,* no. 2, Rotterdam.

Box, G.E.P. and D.A. Pierce, 1970, 'Distribution of residual autocorrelations in autoregressive-integrated moving average time series models', *Journal of the American Statistical Association, 65,* pp. 1509-1526.

Brainard, W.C. and J. Tobin, 1968, 'Pitfalls in financial model building', *American Economic Review, 58,* pp. 99-122.

Brandsma, A. and N. van der Windt, 1980, 'Substitutie op basis van prijzen in de buitenlandse sektor', *Discussion Paper Series* no. 8003/G, Erasmus University, Rotterdam.

Breusch, T.S. and A.R. Pagan, 1980, 'The Lagrange multiplier test and its applications to model specification in econometrics', *Review of Economic Studies, 47,* pp. 239-253.

Butter, F.A.G. den, 1981, 'Monetaire transmissie: een empirische verkenning van de invloed van monetaire grootheden op de bestedingen in Nederland', in: E. den Dunnen, M.M.G. Fase, A. Szász, eds. *Zoeklicht op Beleid,* Stenfert Kroese, Leyden/Antwerp, pp. 83-109.

Butter, F.A.G. den, A.M. Dongelmans and M.M.G. Fase, 1977, 'De vraag naar hypothecair krediet en de rentevorming op de hypotheekmarkt', *De Economist, 125,* pp. 43-74.

Butter, F.A.G. den and M.M.G. Fase, 1981, 'The demand for money in EEC countries', *Journal of Monetary Economics, 8,* pp. 201-230.

Butter, F.A.G. den, M.M.G. Fase and A.P. Huijser, 1979, 'Het netto buitenlands actief van de handelsbanken: een econometrische analyse voor Nederland 1960:II-1975:IV', *Maandschrift Economie, 43,* pp. 161-190.

Centraal Planbureau, 1971, 'Het jaarmodel 1969', in: *Centraal Economisch Plan 1971,* Staatsuitgeverij, The Hague, pp. 181-201.

Centraal Planbureau, 1977, 'Een macro model voor de Nederlandse economie op middellange termijn (VINTAF-II)', *Occasional Paper* no. 12, The Hague.

Conrad, K., 1980, 'An application of duality theory: a portfolio composition of the West-German private non-banking sector '68-'75', *European Economic Review, 13,* pp. 163-189.

Driehuis, W., 1972, *Fluctuations and growth in a near full employment economy,* Rotterdam University Press, Rotterdam.

Duisenberg, W.F., 1984, 'Twee monetaire modellen voor Nederland: overeenkomsten en verschillen tussen de modellen van CPB en DNB', in: H. den Hartog and J. Weitenberg, eds. *Toegepaste Economie: grenzen en mogelijkheden, opstellen aangeboden aan prof. dr. C.A. van den Beld,* Centraal Planbureau, The Hague, pp. 103-114.

Fair, R.C., 1976, *A Model of Macroeconomic Activity,* Ballinger, Cambridge.

Fase, M.M.G., 1977, 'Spaargelden, termijndeposito's en renteverschillen: een econometrische analyse', *Kwartaalbericht De Nederlandsche Bank N.V.,* no. 1, pp. 34-44.

Fase, M.M.G., 1978, 'Een verdeelmodel voor liquide activa', *Economisch Statistische Berichten, 63,* pp. 215-218.

Fase, M.M.G., 1979a, 'The demand for bank credit and the commercial bank lending rate', *De Nederlandsche Bank N.V., Research report* no. 7710 (revised version May 1979).

Fase, M.M.G., 1979b, 'The demand for financial assets', *European Economic Review, 12,* pp. 381-394.

Fase, M.M.G., 1981a, 'Financiële activa, rentevorming en monetaire beheersbaarheid: een proeve van een monetair kwartaalmodel voor Nederland', in: E. den Dunnen, M.M.G. Fase, A. Szász, eds. *Zoeklicht op Beleid,* Stenfert Kroese, Leyden/Antwerp, pp. 43-81.

Fase, M.M.G., 1981b, *Op het breukvlak van macro- en micro-economie,* Stenfert Kroese, Leyden/Antwerp.

Fase, M.M.G., 1982, 'Een reëel kwartaalmodel voor Nederland, REKMON-1-82', *De Nederlandsche Bank N.V., Research report* no. 8204.

Fase, M.M.G., 1984, 'The monetary sector of the Netherlands in 50 equations: a quarterly model for the Netherlands 1970-1979', in: J.P. Ancot, ed. *Analysing the structure of econometric models,* Martinus Nijhoff, The Hague/Boston, pp. 195-228.

Fase, M.M.G., F.A.G. den Butter, R.L. Coenen and M. van Nieuwkerk, 1976, 'Kwartaalmodel voor Nederland: een analyse van en experiment met het kwartaalmodel van het CPB', *De Nederlandsche Bank N.V., Research report* no. 7612.

Fase, M.M.G. and A.P. Huijser, 1980, 'A reaction function for foreign exchange intervention in the Netherlands', *Kredit und Kapital, 6,* pp. 290-319.

Fase, M.M.G. and J.B. Kuné, 1974, 'De vraag naar liquiditeiten in Nederland, 1952-1971, *De Economist, 122,* pp. 326-356.

Fase, M.M.G. and M. van Nieuwkerk, 1975, 'Anticipated inflation and interest rates in an open economy: A study of the Gibson paradox for the Netherlands', in: F. Masera, A. Fazio, T. Padoa-Schioppa, eds. *Econometric Research in European Central Banks, Banca d'Italia,* Rome, pp. 297-321.

Geest, L. van der, 1983, 'Een tijdbom onder de econometrie I en II', *Economisch Statistische Berichten, 68,* p. 741 and p. 761.

Groot, W. and J.J.L.M. Janssen, 1979, 'Goederenuit- en invoer: een empirisch onderzoek', *Ministerie van Economische Zaken, Discussienota* no. 7901.

Hasselman, B.H., V.R. Okker and R.J.A. den Haan, 1983, *FREIA: Een macro-economisch model voor de middellange termijn,* Monografie 25, Centraal Planbureau, The Hague.

Helliwell, J., H. Shapiro, G. Sparks, I. Stewart, F. Gorbet and D. Stephenson, 1971, 'The structure of RDX2, part I', *Bank of Canada, Staff Research Studies* no. 7.

Hendry, D.F., 1979, 'Predictive failure and econometric modelling in macroeconomics: the transactions demand for money', in: P. Ormerod, ed. *Economic Modelling, Current Issues and Problems in Macroeconomic Modelling in the UK and the US,* National Institute for Economic and Social Research, Heinemann, London, pp. 217-242.

Hendry, D.F., 1983, 'Econometric modelling: the consumption function in retrospect', *Scottish Journal of Political Economy, 30,* pp. 193-220.

Hendry, D.F. and J.F. Richard, 1983, 'The econometric analysis of economic time series (with discussion)', *International Statistical Review, 51,* pp. 111-163.

Hennipman, P., 1958, 'Recente kritiek op de economische wetenschap', *Tijdschrift voor Documentatie en Voorlichting, 33,* pp. 249-268.

Hennipman, P., 1962, 'Doeleinden en criteria der economische politiek', in: J.E. Andriessen and M.A.G. Meerhaeghe, eds. *Theorie van de economische politiek,* Stenfert Kroese, Leyden, pp. 1-106.

Huijser, A.P., 1980, 'De samenhang tussen de geldmarkt en de valutamarkt: een eenvoudig structuurmodel', *Maandschrift Economie, 44,* pp. 291-307.

Huijser, A.P., 1984, 'Het kapitaalverkeer van de private sector; een gedesaggregeerd model voor de periode 1970-1980', *Maandschrift Economie, 48,* pp. 175-192.

Huijser, A.P. and P. Kramer, 1979, 'Lonen en extern evenwicht - simulaties met Vintaf II', *De Nederlandsche Bank N.V., Research report* no. 7908.

Imhülsen, D.A., 1981, 'De kleine letters', in: E. den Dunnen, M.M.G. Fase, A. Szász, eds. *Zoeklicht op Beleid,* Stenfert Kroese, Leyden/Antwerp, pp. 151-172.

Keynes, J.M., 1939, 'Prof. Tinbergens method', *Economic Journal, 49,* pp. 558-568.

Kiviet, J.F., 1983, 'On the rigour of some misspecification tests for modelling dynamic relationships', *Faculty of Actuarial Science and Econometrics Report,* AE 11/81 (revised version), University of Amsterdam.

Kiviet, J.F., 1984, 'Model selection tests procedures in a single linear equation of a dynamic simultaneous system and their defects in small samples', *Faculty of Actuarial Science and Econometrics Report,* AE 5/84, University of Amsterdam.

Klant, J.J., 1979, 'De methodologie van J.M. Keynes', in: J.J. Klant, W. Driehuis, H.J. Bierens and A.J. Butter, eds. *Samenleving en Onderzoek,* Stenfert Kroese, Leyden/ Antwerp, pp. 403-411.

Kloek, T., 1984, 'Dynamic adjustment when the target is nonstationary', *International Economic Review, 25,* pp. 315-326.

Knoester, A., 1977, 'Buitenlandse handel, handelskredieten en Zijlstra-effect', *Maandschrift Economie, 41,* no. 7, pp. 319-328.

Knoester, A., 1980, *Over geld en economische politiek,* Stenfert Kroese, Leyden/Antwerp.

Koning, J., 1974, 'Netherlands company pension funds international portfolio diversification', *European Economic Review, 5,* pp. 245-262.

Kramer, P., 1979, 'Twijfels rond de afwenteling in het model VINTAF-II', *Economisch Statistische Berichten, 64,* pp. 1221-1227.

Ljung, G.M. and G.E.P. Box, 1978, 'On a measure of lack of fit in time series models', *Biometrika,* 65, pp. 197-303.

Loo, P.D. van, 1983, *A sectoral analysis of the Dutch financial system,* Stenfert Kroese, Leyden/Antwerp.

Loo, P.D. van, 1984, 'De hoogte van de kapitaalmarktrente', *Maandschrift Economie, 48,* pp. 123-139.

Lucas, R.E., 1976, 'Econometric policy evaluation: a critique', in: K. Brunner and A.H. Meltzer, ed. The Phillips curve and labour markets, *Journal of Monetary Economics,* Supplement no. 1, pp. 19-46.

De Nederlandsche Bank N.V., 1982, *Kwartaalconfrontatie van middelen en bestedingen 1957-1980,* Kluwer, Deventer.

Nieuwkerk, M. van, 1978, *Determinanten van het handelskrediet,* Amsterdam.

Patinkin, D., 1976, 'Keynes and econometrics: on the interaction between the macroeconomic revolutions of the interwar period', *Econometrica, 44,* pp. 1091-1123.

Pen, J., 1984, 'Homo economicus', *Hollands Maandblad, 26,* pp. 23-30.

Saito, M., 1977, 'Household flow-of-funds equation: specification and estimation', *Journal of Money, Credit and Banking, 9,* pp. 1-20.

Sandee, J., 1966, 'Schatten, toetsen en beslissen in de macro-economie', *De Economist, 114,* pp. 473-484.

Sargent, Th. J., 1976, 'A classical macroeconometric model for the United States', *Journal of Political Economy, 84,* pp. 207-237.

Sargent, Th. J. and N. Wallace, 1975, 'Rational expectations, the optimal monetary instrument and the optimal money supply rule', *Journal of Political Economy, 83,* pp. 241-254.

Straaten, A.J. van, 1981, 'Liquiditeit en liquiditeiten', in: E. den Dunnen, M.M.G. Fase , A. Szász, eds. *Zoeklicht op Beleid,* Stenfert Kroese, Leyden/Antwerp, pp. 111-140.

Taylor, J.C. and K.W. Clements, 1983, 'A simple portfolio allocation model of financial wealth', *European Economic Review, 23,* pp. 241-251.

Name Index

Subject Index

GPSR Compliance

The European Union's (EU) General Product Safety Regulation (GPSR) is a set of rules that requires consumer products to be safe and our obligations to ensure this.

If you have any concerns about our products, you can contact us on ProductSafety@springernature.com

In case Publisher is established outside the EU, the EU authorized representative is:

Springer Nature Customer Service Center GmbH
Europaplatz 3
69115 Heidelberg, Germany

Batch number: 10824729

Printed by Printforce, the Netherlands